HOMESPUN
CRAFTS
FROM SCRAPS

Opposite, clockwise from top: Lollipop Christmas Tree Ornaments, p. 84; Pinecone Christmas Wreath, p. 95; Patchwork Christmas Tree Skirt, p. 89.

Above, clockwise from top: Child's Rainbow Stocking Cap, p. 104; Tulip-Painted Mirror, p. 45; Child's Rainbow Legwarmers, p. 108.

Below left: Basket Doll Cradle, p. 119; *right:* Child's Sail-Away Wall Hanging, p. 128.

Book jacket front, clockwise from left: Eight-Pointed Star Pillow, p. 65; Sunny Coffee-Can Organizer, p. 140; Footlocker/Wooden Chest Coffee Table, p. 25.
Half title page, clockwise from top: Stenciled Welcome Sign, p. 76; Dresden Plate Pillow, p. 71; Beribboned Band Boxes, p. 151; Colonial Lap Desk, p. 38.

Left: Woodlands Pinecone Heart, p. 92; *right:* Mushroom Basket Centerpiece, p. 145.

Clockwise from top: Calico House Portrait, p. 80; Windowsill Planter, p. 18; Patchwork Points Table Runner, p. 42.

Opposite, clockwise from top: Christmas Card Wreath, p. 87; Calico-Lined Basket, p. 21; Patchwork Christmas Tablecloth, p. 99; Quilted Tea Cozy and Potholder, p. 61.

Opposite, left: Child's Painting Smock, p. 113; *right from top:* Heart Potholder, p. 49; Whale Potholder, p. 53; Calico Tulip Potholder, p. 57.

Clockwise from top: Seashell Mobile, p. 142; Calico-Covered Desk Set, p. 33.

Left: Little Helper's Tool Apron, p. 124; *right:* Boutique Bath Hanger, p. 30.

Clockwise from left: Calico Collage, p. 147; Red Plaid Baby Bunting, p. 133; Calico-Covered Sweetheart Frame, p. 155.

HOMESPUN CRAFTS FROM SCRAPS

HOMESPUN CRAFTS FROM SCRAPS

GWEN EVRARD

A Genie Book

New Century Publishers, Inc.

JACKET AND BOOK DESIGN BY JESSICA WEBER

PHOTOGRAPHY BY ERNIE SILVA

EDITED BY LINDA McCLOW

11 12 13 14 15 16

ISBN 0-8329-0253-5

Library of Congress Cataloging in Publication Data

Evrard, Gwen.
   Homespun crafts from scraps.

   "A Genie book."
   Includes index.
   1. Handicraft.   2. Waste products.   3. Recycling
(Waste, etc.)   I. Title
TT157.E93   1983   745.58′4   82-18832
ISBN 0-8329-0253-5

Printed in the United States of America

AUTHOR'S GUARANTEE

Every effort has been made to ensure the accuracy
and clarity of the directions in this book. Although
we cannot be responsible for misinterpretation of
directions or variations caused by the individual's
working techniques, we would be happy to answer
any questions you may have about the directions.
Address inquiries to the author, in care of:

Genie Books
218 Madison Avenue
New York, N.Y. 10016

With love to my mother,
from whom I inherited my creativity

ACKNOWLEDGMENTS

Putting a book together is never a one-person operation. Several people were instrumental in getting this one to the presses, and I'd like to share my appreciation with them.

I'd like to thank my aunt Eleanor Coombes for making the boutique bath hanger, Joan Nusser for working up the knitted projects, and Chris Nolan for lending back to me the calico house portrait.

To Marilyn Dodd, whose creativity is exceptional, a giant round of applause for all the work she did on eight of the projects.

Thanks also to my mother, who took on the huge job of typing this manuscript.

My love and gratitude to my husband, Tom, and my children, Lauren and Thomas, who lived with wood chips and fabric scraps flying. An extra thank-you to Lauren for making the calico collage project.

Finally, a special thank-you to Jeanne McClow, whose praise and confidence in my work helps to make my creativity flow.

CONTENTS

Let's Get Organized

Around the House

Holiday Ideas

For the Children

By the Children

INTRODUCTION

For me, craftworking has become a very pleasant way to spend my spare time. One of the reasons for this book was to share some of that pleasure with you, the reader/craftsperson. But the main reason was to create projects that could be made inexpensively by recycling and yet that were of a good-enough design that anyone would be proud to own them himself or to give them as gifts to some special person. Even if you don't have the materials on hand to make these projects and have to buy them, the end results will all be well worth the small monetary investment. The projects are all of a country style updated with 1980s chic, they are creative without being cute, and they range from being functional to purely decorative. The designs are fresh, and through making them, you'll be given a new slant on many familiar craft techniques.

This book was written to be used by the whole family. The variety of projects incorporates many kinds of craft work and will attract just about anyone who enjoys making things. Some of the techniques we have used are sewing, stenciling, woodworking, knitting, quilting, and embroidering. (There is a guide in the beginning of the book to help to familiarize you with some of the techniques you may not have tried before.) There are projects for the children to make, such as the calico collage, and more complicated ones for the accomplished craftsperson to tackle, such as the appliquéd house portrait. Some of the projects are suitable for more than one person to work on. For instance, one person might want to do the woodworking on the hand-painted mirror frame, while another might do the decorative painting on it. The principle of the whole family joining in reminds me of the days gone by, when everyone gathered around the fire in the evening to do handwork. I'd be happy if this book were to bring a little of that togetherness back into our lives.

A special concept of this book is that each of the projects was designed and made with you in mind. The ease and attractiveness of country-style decorating has made itself known to all of us for its warmth and simplicity, and the projects in the book reflect our love of that style, which we inherited from our forefathers. They developed it out of need, and it manifested itself in many ways, such as quilting and patchworking to make use of every precious bit of fabric, simple woodworking in keeping with the simple tools available, and stenciling in place of mass-produced decorating. Mass-production had not yet tainted the quality of these items, made so lovingly, and each one differed slightly from the next as a result of being made by hand. Many of the projects in this book can be personalized in this one-of-a-kind manner, by using your own color schemes and decorative designs. Use our projects and directions as guides and let your own style and imagination take over—the finished projects should bear your own stamp of creativity.

And so this book was written for you—to help you bring quality craft work into your home; to enable you to shape and create country-style projects with the people you love; and to guide you into letting your creativity and craft work shine. By the way, you'll have lots of fun using the book, too—that's as important a reason as any.

ABOUT
THE TOOLS
AND MATERIALS

Most of the tools and materials used in our projects are likely to be found around your home right now, especially if you have previously done any type of craft work. In some cases, you may want to substitute a tool or material you have on hand for one we have specified. Since any craft project is a form of art, there are no strict rules, and, of course, using materials on hand can save you money. Just use our tools, materials, and procedures as guidelines for each project, and let your imagination do the rest.

The following alphabetical list is included to give an expanded view of some of the less-familiar tools and materials.

Baby's breath: A dried flower sold in florist shops, nurseries, garden centers, and craft-supply stores. Available in bunches, it has small, white, delicate flowers on sticklike stems.

Corner guard molding: This wood molding, which is as deep as it is wide, is usually used to protect paint and wallpaper in doorways, but it gives a trim finish when used as framing.

Corrugated wood fasteners: These wood fasteners, which come in several different sizes, are used to connect two pieces of wood. Their wavy shape is designed to prevent the joined pieces from slipping apart.

Fabric fuser: There are several brands of fabric fuser on the market, among them Stitch Witchery and Jiffy Fuse. Available in notions and fabric departments, the fuser is placed between two pieces of fabric, wrong sides together, and pressed together with a hot iron (when cutting the pieces, cut the fabric slightly larger than the fuser). Fusing fabric in this way gives greater strength to the fabric, helps prevent the edges from fraying, and enables you to have two right sides to the fabric.

Fabric marker: There are several kinds of fabric markers and pencils available in sewing and notions departments. There is also a felt-tipped marker that is water-soluble available on the market.

Florist's wire: Florist's wire, which is used in floral arrangements, is thin, flexible, and coated with a green substance so that it is as invisible as possible.

Latex paint: This is rubber-based, water-soluble paint, which can be used for either interior or exterior painting. It is ideal for wood and it can be easily cleaned with soap and water.

Metal wreath ring: This type of ring, which is used to make straw, pinecone, and evergreen wreaths, is available in a variety of sizes at garden centers and craft-supply stores.

Miter box: This wood or plastic tool, available at hardware stores, is used to hold a saw at an angle for cutting wood and molding that is to be joined at corners. Because both angles of a corner can be cut to exactly the same degree with a miter box, the pieces to be joined are assured of fitting together snugly.

Polyester stuffing: This washable, light-weight material is usually sold in one- or two-pound packs. The one-pound size is sufficient to fill a 12- to 18-inch-square pillow.

Quilt batting: Batting is a flat, layered filling used between the layers of fabric in comforters or quilts. It is sold in rolls of assorted sizes and is washable and light-weight. Years ago, sewers used batting made of cotton, but today it is available in polyester, which is lighter in weight and dries more quickly.

Quilting needles: Smaller than sewing needles, quilting needles enable smaller stitches to be taken. The size we recommend is either size 7 or 8.

Quilting thread: This strong thread is coated with a waxy finish to help prevent it from knotting and tangling when quilting.

Seam ripper: This pointed tool, available in notions departments, has a sharp edge used for cutting through stitches.

Stencil paper: Technically, stencil paper is a heavy-weight paper with a waxy coating used to cut stencils. You can, however, also cut stencils out of cardboard, acetate, or heavy paper.

Straw flowers: These dried flowers, available in many sizes and colors at garden centers and craft stores, retain their colors and shapes for a long time, so that they are ideal for use in floral arrangements and on wreaths.

Tailor's chalk: This thin square of chalk, available in notions departments, is used by tailors to mark fabrics.

Velcro: This double-faced tape, which is used to join two surfaces, has one side covered with a plastic pile and one side covered with plastic loops. When these two surfaces are pressed together, they adhere to each other. Velcro is used on sewing projects in place of snaps, buttons, or zippers. It is available wherever sewing supplies are sold.

White glue: When a project calls for white glue, use a water-soluble glue, such as Elmer's. This glue is available in stationery, hardware, craft, and large grocery stores.

Wood filler: This material, which is available at hardware stores and lumberyards, is used to fill small holes and cracks in wood. After application, this initially soft material hardens and can be sandpapered smooth. You can then paint or finish it just as you would a piece of wood.

Wooden dowels: Wooden dowels are cylindrical wood rods that come in various diameters from $1/8$ inch to 2 inches. They are often used in craft work and are available at lumberyards and craft stores.

PROCEDURES

Below we have given the basic steps for some of the crafts involved in making the projects in the book in order to simplify them for you. It would be impossible to go into each of these in depth, since each one alone could fill a book, but what you learn here might be an introduction to an area that you might want to explore more thoroughly.

APPLIQUÉING

The technique of appliqué is actually sewing a fabric shape to a fabric background.

A. Place the fabric from which you will cut the appliqué right side up on a flat surface. Place the pattern for the appliqué on top of it and trace around it. Cut the appliqué shape out of the fabric, allowing ¼ inch extra all around to allow for the raw edges to be turned under before stitching the appliqué in place. Turn the raw edges toward the wrong side of the fabric along the traced line, and baste them in place (Diagram 1).

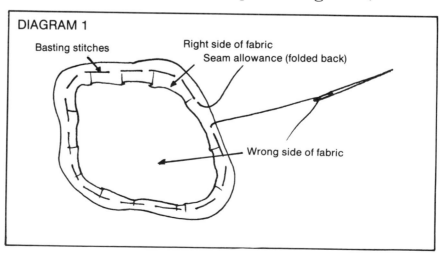

DIAGRAM 1

Basting stitches

Right side of fabric

Seam allowance (folded back)

Wrong side of fabric

11

B. Right side up, pin the basted appliqué shape in place to the right side of the fabric. Baste the appliqué in place and remove the pins.

C. Thread a sewing needle with a single thread and tie a knot in the end. To stitch the appliqué in place, push the needle up from the wrong side of the fabric just at the edge of the appliqué (Diagram 2).

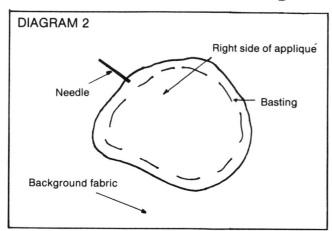

DIAGRAM 2

Right side of appliqué

Needle

Basting

Background fabric

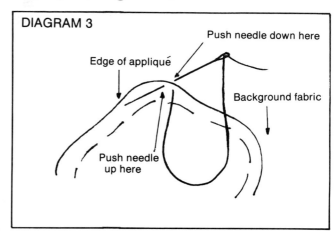

DIAGRAM 3

Push needle down here

Edge of appliqué

Background fabric

Push needle up here

Pull the thread all the way through and then push the needle down through the background fabric close to the edge of the appliqué. Bring the needle back up through the edge of the appliqué about ⅛ inch away from the first stitch (Diagram 3).

Repeat the stitches until the appliqué is attached all the way around.

EMBROIDERING

The embroidery work in this book is done with two strands of cotton embroidery floss. We have used only two kinds of stitches on the projects—the outline stitch and the satin stitch. Both are diagrammed below.

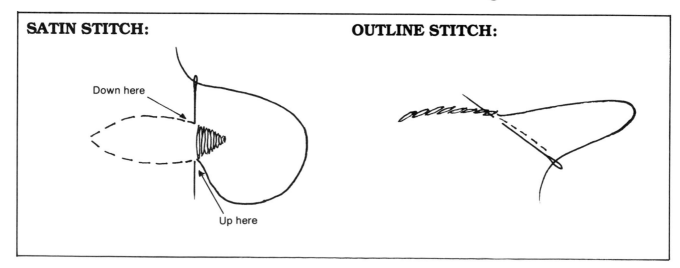

SATIN STITCH:

Down here

Up here

OUTLINE STITCH:

ENLARGING PATTERNS

Many of the patterns in this book need to be enlarged since there was not space to reproduce them in full size. The patterns that need to be enlarged are reduced on a grid. The following steps describe how to enlarge the patterns.

A. On a sheet of brown wrapping paper or other paper—even newspaper will work—draw a grid of 1-inch boxes, making as many boxes across and down as there are on the grid over the pattern you are enlarging.

B. Working square by square, transfer the pattern to the larger grid by copying the lines in each box of the smaller grid to each box of the larger grid.

MITERING CORNERS WITH WOOD

To make a wood frame, such as for the Tulip-Painted Mirror, you must cut the ends of the wood at equal angles so that they will fit together. This process is called mitering. To do this, you will need a tool known as a miter box, which is available in any hardware store or department store. You will also need a handsaw, a pencil, and a ruler. Follow the steps below for mitering wood.

A. Decide how long and how wide you want the final project to be. Add 4 inches to each of these measurements and cut two pieces of wood to each of these measurements.

B. Place one of the pieces of wood into the miter box. Place the saw on an angle in the slots of the miter box. Be sure the angle you are going to cut starts out at one of the corners of the piece of wood (Diagram 1). Saw the end of the wood off at this angle.

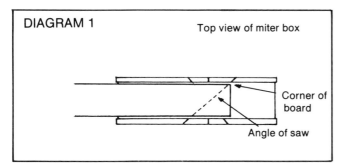

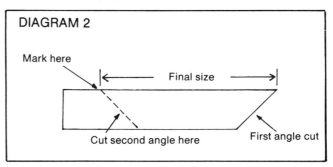

C. Measure the final size along the top edge of the wood. (The top edge will be the longest part of the wood.) Mark the length with a pencil (Diagram 2).

Place the wood in the miter box to cut the angle at the opposite end. Line the pencil mark up so that the angle goes from that point in to the lower point and saw through it (Diagram 2).

13

D. Repeat this procedure with the other three pieces of wood for the frame. (*Note:* If you are cutting corner molding, you need only to cut the front angles correctly for the side edges to be cut correctly [Diagram 3].)

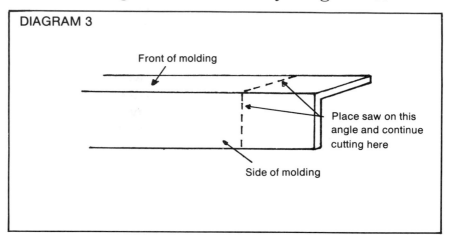

DIAGRAM 3

Front of molding

Place saw on this angle and continue cutting here

Side of molding

QUILTING

Quilting is actually the joining of two or more layers of fabric together with tiny running stitches. In this book, all quilting projects join three layers together—backing, batting, and a front fabric. The following steps explain how to do basic quilting.

A. Pin the three layers to be quilted together, starting in the center and working out to the edges in eight directions (Diagram 1). By working from the center out, any wrinkles can be smoothed out at the edges of the fabric. Baste along the pin lines and remove the pins.

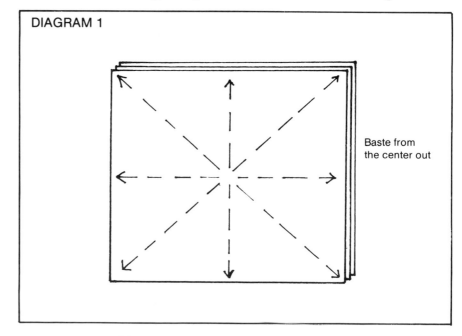

DIAGRAM 1

Baste from the center out

B. Thread the quilting needle with a single strand of quilting thread 30 to 36 inches long. Tie a small knot at the end of the thread. Push the needle up from the back of the fabric to the spot where you want to start quilting. Pull the thread gently but firmly enough that the knot pulls through the backing fabric only and will be concealed between the layers of the batting and fabric.

C. Take two tiny stitches through all three layers and pull the thread all the way through the fabric. Continue taking tiny stitches until you have finished the line of quilting or until the thread is running out. Then push the needle down through the top layer of fabric and bring it back up through the top layer about ¾ inch away. Cut the thread next to the fabric. The end will disappear into the layers of fabric. There should be 6 or 7 quilting stitches per inch on top of the fabric and the stitches should be as uniform in size as possible.

SLIP STITCHING

Many of the projects in this book require an opening to be closed with a slip stitch. This is a tiny stitch, taken as invisibly as possible, that is used to close a seam. The diagram below illustrates how to do slip stitches.

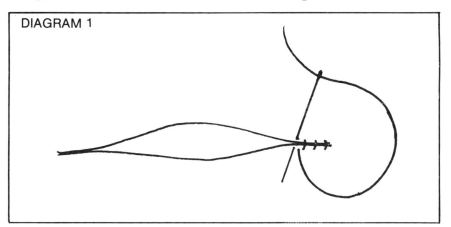

DIAGRAM 1

STENCILING

Like many crafts, stenciling can be very simple or very complex. For our purposes we have kept it very simple.

Our stencils can be cut from acetate or stencil paper, both of which are available at craft stores. You can also use cardboard or heavy paper if you wish. The designs can be cut with single-edged razor blades or X-acto knives. The X-acto knife has a cylinder-shaped handle about the size of a pencil that can be fitted with a variety of sharp, pointed blades. X-acto knives are available at hardware, art-supply, and craft stores. When you are using these tools, be sure to cut clean, crisp lines for best results.

To fill in the stencil, we find that acrylic paints work well, especially for someone who has not done much stenciling work. They dry quickly, are available in many colors, and clean up with soap and water. Latex paints and oil paints can also be used for the stenciling in this book.

The stenciling itself can be done with sponges, stencil brushes, or a piece of velvet wrapped around your finger and dipped into the paint. Whatever you use, it should be fairly dry so that the paint won't run under the edges of the stencil. Try dabbing on a piece of newspaper before beginning to stencil to remove excess paint.

To begin stenciling, tape the stencil to the piece you are stenciling and then gently dab the sponge, brush, or velvet over the cutouts, using an up-and-down motion and pressing down on the edges of the cutouts to help prevent seepage. When you have finished stenciling an area, let the paint set for a minute and then carefully lift the stencil straight up so that it will not smudge the paint.

TRANSFERRING PATTERNS

The patterns for the projects will have to be transferred to whatever materials you are working on. The first step is to trace the pattern from the book on a piece of paper. To transfer it to wood or a painted surface, place a piece of graphite paper (available at art-supply or craft stores), carbon paper, or chalk-backed paper face down on the surface to which the design is to be transferred. Place the paper with the pattern on top of it and trace around the lines of the pattern with a pencil.

To transfer a pattern to fabric, simply cut the pattern out of the paper and pin it to the fabric. Cut or trace around the pattern, according to the individual project directions.

To transfer lines to be embroidered, rub chalk on the back of the pattern to be transferred. Place the pattern on the fabric and trace over the lines to transfer the chalk lines to the fabric.

1

LET'S GET ORGANIZED

WINDOWSILL PLANTER

Give your plants loving care in this windowsill planter adorned with plump hearts. It is an ideal holder for your kitchen herb plants, or, set in a sunny spot, it is a good place to start seedlings. It can also be used to group small houseplants. The planter is not meant to be planted in directly; it is conveniently sized to hold two disposable loaf pans, or you can cut the bottoms off milk cartons or yogurt containers, fill each with a plant, and then set them into the planter.

MATERIALS

scrap lumber, ¾ inch thick
ruler
pencil
handsaw
hammer
wire nails, 1 inch long
sandpaper for wood, medium grade
paintbrush, 1½ inches wide
latex housepaint, in colonial blue or the color of your choice
brown wrapping paper or other paper for cutting pattern
piece of heavy cardboard, about 4 by 4 inches
acrylic paint, in white
small paintbrush
2 disposable aluminum-foil loaf pans (optional), each 2½ by 3½ by 8 inches

PROCEDURE

1. Cut the lumber scraps to the following measurements: one piece 5½ by 19¾ inches; two pieces 5½ by 3⅜ inches; and two pieces 3⅜ by 21¼ inches.

2. Nail one of the 5½-inch edges of each of the two smallest pieces of wood to the short ends of the 5½- by 19¾-inch piece, as shown in Diagram 1.

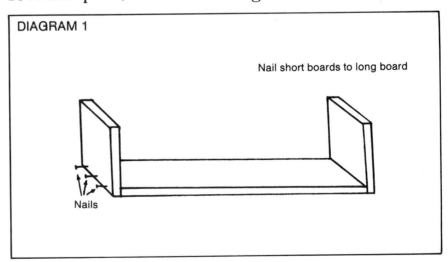

DIAGRAM 1

Nail short boards to long board

Nails

3. Nail the two 3⅜- by 21¼-inch pieces of wood to the long sides of the 5½- by 19¾-inch piece, lining the edges up with the short end pieces (Diagram 2).

4. Lightly sand the planter with the sandpaper.

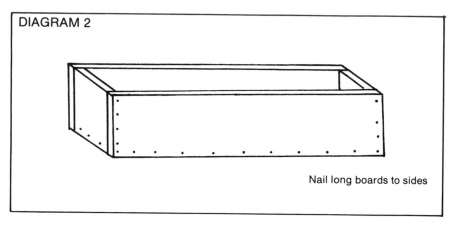

DIAGRAM 2

Nail long boards to sides

5. Paint the planter with the 1½-inch-wide paintbrush and the housepaint. Allow the paint to dry according to manufacturer's directions and give the planter a second coat of paint; allow the paint to dry.

6. With the brown wrapping paper, ruler, and pencil, enlarge the pattern for the heart shape (see p. 13). Cut the pattern out of the paper and place it on top of the cardboard. Trace around it and remove the paper pattern. Cut the pattern out of the cardboard.

7. Following the project photograph for placement, center the cardboard pattern on one of the long sides of the planter and trace around it. Repeat this step on the other three sides of the planter.

8. Paint in the heart shapes with the white acrylic paint and the small paintbrush. Allow the paint to dry. Add the loaf pans if desired and fill with plants.

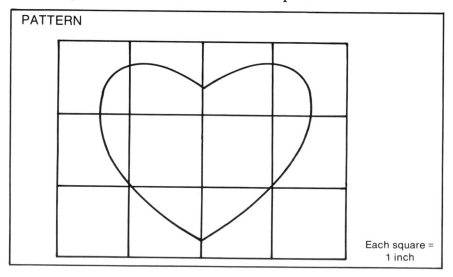

PATTERN

Each square = 1 inch

2

CALICO-LINED BASKET

Pretty-up a wicker basket with this ruffled calico lining and heap it with fresh hot rolls from the oven for your dinner table, or use it to hold your knitting, crocheting, or needlepoint, or fill it with your sewing supplies—the lining, which can be untied and tossed in the washing machine, serves to keep things from slipping through the wicker and at the same time adds a charming decorative touch. Because every basket varies in size, you'll need to adjust the measurements we give to those of your basket.

MATERIALS

rectangular-shaped wicker basket with a handle
ruler
pencil
½ yard calico fabric
scissors
straight pins
thread in color to match fabric
needle

PROCEDURE

1. Measure the outside surfaces of the basket—the sides, ends, and the bottom (Diagram 1). Cut two rectangles of fabric to each set of measurements. (It is not necessary to add extra for seam allowances because you measured the outside of the basket.)

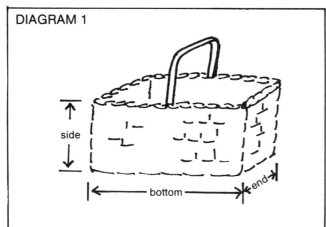

DIAGRAM 1

side

bottom

end

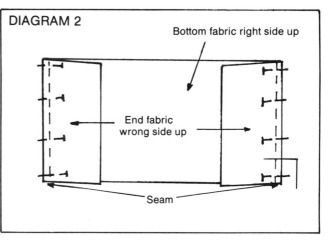

DIAGRAM 2

Bottom fabric right side up

End fabric
wrong side up

Seam

2. Place one of the pieces you have cut for the bottom on a flat surface with the right side of the fabric facing up. With right sides of the fabric facing, pin one of the pieces cut for the end to each short edge, as shown in Diagram 2. Stitch the ends to the bottom with a ¼-inch seam allowance and remove the pins.

3. Fold the end pieces out and, with right sides of the fabric facing, pin the side pieces to the bottom piece (Diagram 3). Stitch the side piece to the bottom with a ¼-inch seam allowance and remove the pins.

4. Bring two adjoining pieces of the fabric up to meet at one corner and, with right sides facing, pin them to each other. Stitch the seam together with a ¼-inch seam allowance (Diagram 4) and remove the pins. Repeat this with the other three corners. This is one of the lining pieces. Set this piece aside.

5. Repeat steps 2, 3, and 4 with the remaining pieces of fabric. This is the second lining piece.

6. Measure the length and width of the top edges of one of the lining pieces you have just sewn (Diagram 5). Add the measurements together and multiply this number by four.

7. Cut a 1½-inch-wide strip of fabric the length of the number you found in step 6. You may have to cut two pieces and join them together with a seam to get a strip long enough. This is the strip for the pleated ruffle around the top of the lining.

8. Fold the strip in half lengthwise with the right sides together and stitch a ¼-inch seam at the short ends. Turn the strip right side out and press it flat.

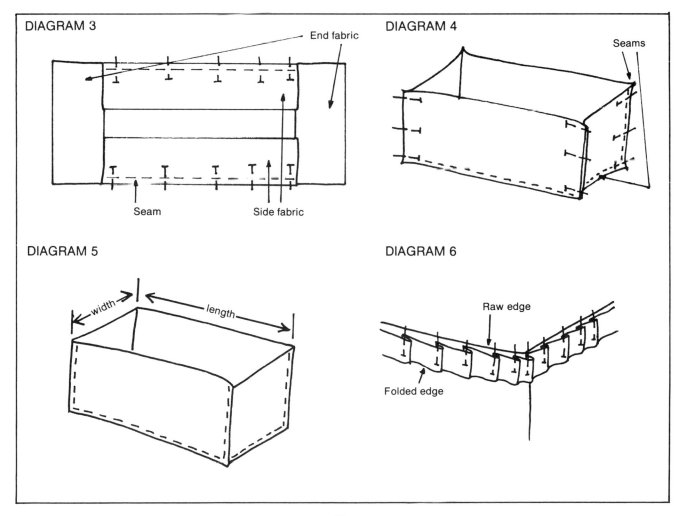

DIAGRAM 3

End fabric

Seam

Side fabric

DIAGRAM 4

Seams

DIAGRAM 5

width

length

DIAGRAM 6

Raw edge

Folded edge

9. With the right sides of the fabric facing and starting in one corner, pin the raw edges of the strip around the top raw edge of one of the lining pieces, making ½-inch pleats as you pin (Diagram 6) and overlapping the ends where they meet in the corner.

10. Stitch the ruffle to the top of the lining with a ¼-inch seam allowance, remove the pins, and turn the ruffles up so that the folded edge is on top.

11. Wrong sides together, set the lining piece with the ruffle sewn to it inside the remaining lining piece (Diagram 7).

12. Fold the top raw edge of the outer lining piece ¼ inch to the wrong side of the fabric all around so that the raw edges at the bottom of the ruffle are concealed between the two lining pieces and slip stitch the outer lining to the edge of the ruffle to join the two pieces of the lining. Remove the pins.

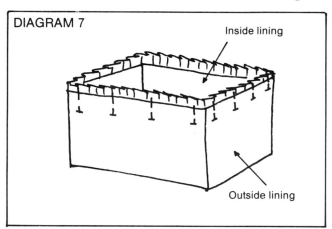

DIAGRAM 7

Inside lining

Outside lining

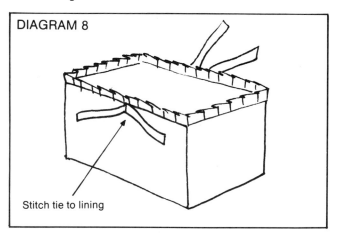

DIAGRAM 8

Stitch tie to lining

13. To make the ties: Cut two strips of fabric, each 2½ by 40 inches. Fold them in half lengthwise with the right sides of the fabric facing. Stitch along one of the short ends and the length of the strip with a ¼-inch seam allowance. Turn the strip right side out through the open end. Tuck the raw ends in ¼ inch and slip stitch the end closed. Repeat with the remaining strip of fabric.

14. Sew one strip to the ruffle in the center of each long side of the lining (Diagram 8).

15. Place the lining inside the basket and tie each strip into a bow around the base of the handle.

3

FOOTLOCKER/ WOODEN-CHEST COFFEE TABLE

Here's a handy coffee table/storage spot that you can make from a shabby footlocker or wooden chest. We rescued an old footlocker for our project, which we painted a colonial blue, added some cheerfully plump Pennsylvania Dutch-style hearts and flowers, as well as the symbol of hospitality—the pineapple, and lined the interior with a colonial wallpaper. The result is a unique folk-art piece that will add country charm to any interior—traditional or contemporary. Since each chest varies slightly in size and hardware, we have given patterns for basic design elements that can be adapted according to your own preferences.

MATERIALS

footlocker or wooden chest
damp cloth
1 quart acrylic housepaint in medium blue
paintbrush, 1½ inches wide
ruler
pencil
single-edged razor blade
enough leftover wallpaper to line the inside of the chest
wallpaper paste (not needed if the wallpaper is
    prepasted)
sponge
brown wrapping paper or other paper for cutting
    pattern
tracing paper for tracing pattern
white chalk
masking tape
fine paintbrush
acrylic paint in black, gold, dark blue, white
small can gloss-finish polyurethane

PROCEDURE

1. Wipe the footlocker or chest inside and out with the damp cloth to remove any dirt and dust and allow it to dry.

2. Using the acrylic housepaint and the 1½-inch-wide paintbrush, paint the outside of the chest and the inside edges of the lid. Allow the chest to dry. (Read the label on the can of paint for correct drying time.) Give the chest a second coat of paint and allow it to dry.

3. Measure the inside top, bottom, and side surfaces of the chest (Diagram 1). Adding 1 inch to the length and depth of the sides, cut rectangles of wallpaper to these measurements, using a razor blade and a ruler.

4. If the wallpaper is not prepasted, mix the wallpaper paste, following the directions on the package. You will not need to use a whole package, so reduce the proportions.

5. Using the sponge to smooth out the wrinkles, paste the wallpaper to the four sides of the chest, overlapping 1 inch on the bottom surface on each side. Paste the wallpaper to the inside bottom surface of the chest and then to the inside top surface of the lid, trimming the edges with a razor blade if necessary for an exact fit.

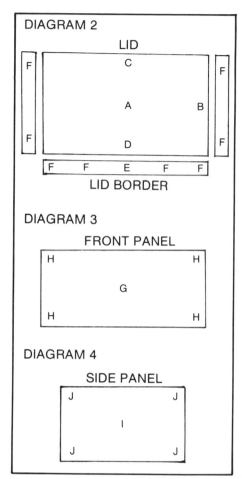

DIAGRAM 2

LID

LID BORDER

DIAGRAM 3

FRONT PANEL

DIAGRAM 4

SIDE PANEL

6. Using the brown wrapping paper, ruler, and pencil, enlarge the decorative patterns (see p. 13).

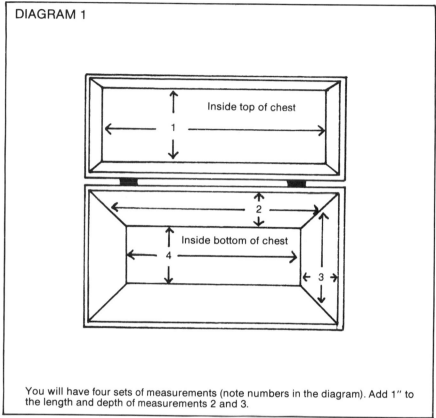

DIAGRAM 1

Inside top of chest

Inside bottom of chest

You will have four sets of measurements (note numbers in the diagram). Add 1″ to the length and depth of measurements 2 and 3.

7. Using the tracing paper and pencil, trace the patterns. Turn the tracings over and rub the back of the tracing with the white chalk, making sure to cover all the areas of the design.

8. Using the project photograph and Diagrams 2, 3, and 4 as guides for the placement of the designs, tape one motif to the trunk with the chalk side against the surface. Trace over the design with a pencil to transfer the motif to the chest.

9. Following the key for colors, paint the design on the chest, using the fine brush and the acrylic paints. We used four colors for the designs on our chest—gold, light gold, light blue, and black. You will have to mix the light gold and the light blue by adding white to the gold and dark blue acrylic paints. All the fine-line highlighting is done in black and should be added using the project photograph as a guide.

10. Continue transferring the designs, being sure to rub the backs of the tracings with chalk each time they are reused, and painting them in. When all have been painted, allow them to dry thoroughly.

11. Using the 1½-inch-wide paintbrush, give the chest two coats of polyurethane, allowing it to dry between coats. (Check the label on the can for proper drying time.)

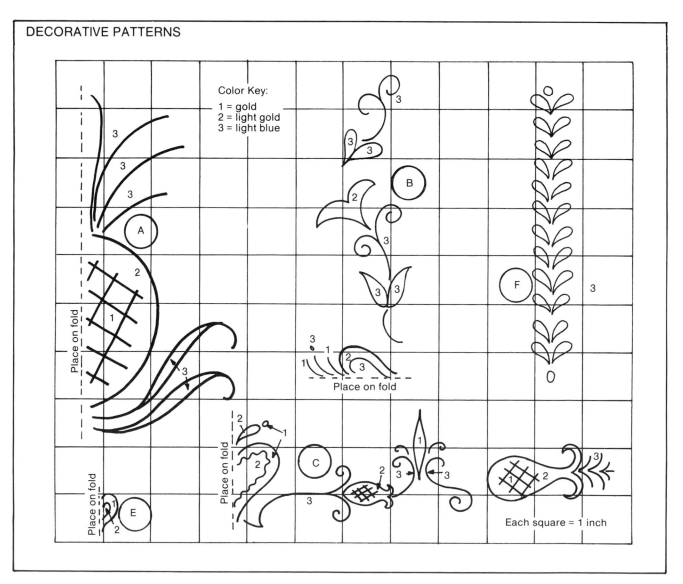

DECORATIVE PATTERNS

Color Key:
1 = gold
2 = light gold
3 = light blue

Place on fold

Place on fold

Place on fold

Place on fold

Each square = 1 inch

DECORATIVE PATTERNS

Place on fold

Place on fold

Place on fold

I

J

D

G

H

Each square = 1 inch

4

BOUTIQUE BATH HANGER

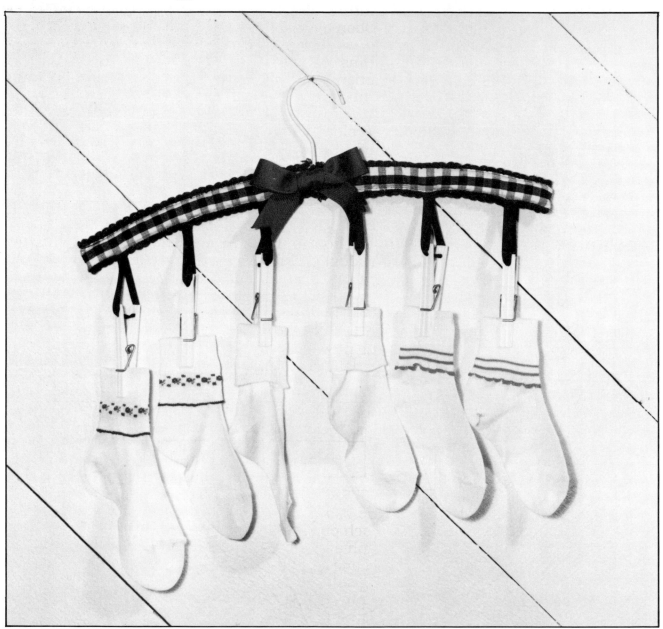

Zip-up your bathroom with this practical but prettily beribboned hanger designed for drying lingerie. Although it would be expensive to purchase in a bath boutique, we will show you how to make one for pennies. These hangers are perfect for bazaars or as small tokens of thanks to friends—try color-coordinating them with your friend's bathroom. You might use satin and lace for a feminine touch or a bold fabric and bright plastic for a contemporary look. Coordinate the ribbon to match your bedroom, omit the clothespins, and you can brighten up your clothes closet with a designer hanger.

MATERIALS

flat wooden hanger without bottom rod
leftover paint (semigloss or gloss, oil-base or latex will
  do) in white
small paintbrush
1 yard ribbon with a crocheted-look edge, 1 inch wide
scissors
straight pins
1 yard ribbon, ¼ inch wide, in color to coordinate with
  ribbon above
needle
thread in color to match crocheted-edge ribbon above
6 pinch-type plastic clothespins with holes in the ends,
  in white
½ yard ribbon, 1 inch wide, in a contrasting color, for
  the bow

PROCEDURE

1. Paint the hook of the hanger with the white paint. (If there is enough paint left in the can, you might dip the hook right into the paint.) Let the paint dry.

2. Cut the 1-inch-wide edged ribbon in half widthwise (Diagram 1). Set one piece aside and work with the remaining piece. Lay the ribbon on a flat surface and mark the halfway point with a pin, as shown in Diagram 1.

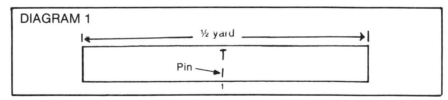

DIAGRAM 1

½ yard

Pin

3. Cut the ¼-inch-wide ribbon into six pieces crosswise so that each piece is 6 inches long. Using the project photograph and Diagram 2 as guides, stitch about ¼ inch of one end of the first length, right side out, to the wrong side of the 1-inch-wide edged ribbon 1 inch from the pin marker. Attach the second piece 2 inches from the first piece and the third piece 2 inches from the second.

4. Thread the end of one of the three pieces of ¼-inch-wide ribbon through both holes of one of the clothespins. Fold the end of the ribbon up, and stitch it over the end you sewed to the 1-inch-wide edged ribbon, as shown in Diagram 3. Repeat this procedure with the next two pieces of ribbon.

5. Wrong sides together, fold the edged ribbon in half widthwise where you marked it with the pin; remove the pin. Sew a ⅛-inch seam along the two long edges, as shown in Diagram 4.

6. Repeat steps 2 through 5 with the remaining ribbon and clothespins.

7. Slide one of the pieces of ribbon with the clothespins attached to it over one half of the hanger. Slide the other piece over the other side of the hanger. Tuck the raw ends of the ribbon in and slip stitch them together in the middle, as shown in Diagram 5.

8. Using the ½ yard of ribbon in the contrasting color, tie a bow and sew it to one of the flat sides of the hanger under the hook.

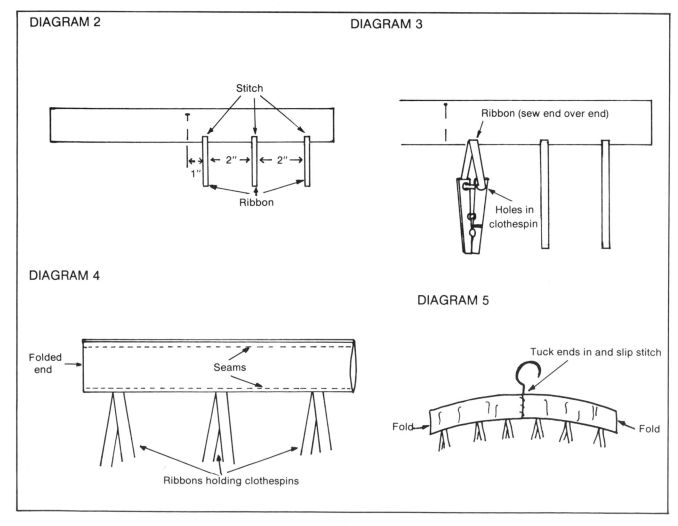

DIAGRAM 2

DIAGRAM 3

Stitch

Ribbon (sew end over end)

Holes in clothespin

2"

2"

1"

Ribbon

DIAGRAM 4

DIAGRAM 5

Folded end

Seams

Tuck ends in and slip stitch

Fold

Fold

Ribbons holding clothespins

5

CALICO-COVERED DESK SET

Liven up a tired old desk set with some spritely calico fabric and bands of satin ribbon. This project, which is really three projects in one—a pencil holder, a cover for a book of personal telephone numbers, and a desk pad— makes a thoughtful gift for a young lady going away to college or, in a plaid fabric, a nice addition to a man's desk. Or color-coordinate it to the rest of your decor and make it for yourself.

MATERIALS

1 yard calico fabric, 45 inches wide
1 yard fabric fuser (such as Jiffy Fuse or Stitch Witchery)
ruler
scissors
white glue
1 frozen-juice-concentrate can, 12-ounce size
brown wrapping paper
64 inches ribbon, ⅜ inch wide, in color to coordinate with fabric above
personal telephone-number book, 5½ by 7 inches, with slip-in directory pages (this is a style readily available at stationery stores)
2 pieces heavy paper, each 4½ by 6 inches, in white
desk pad, 12 by 19 inches
piece of blotter paper in color to coordinate with fabric

PROCEDURE

PENCIL HOLDER

1. With wrong sides together, fold the fabric in half widthwise. Cut the fabric in half along the fold (Diagram 1). Use the fabric fuser to join the two pieces of fabric, following manufacturer's directions.

2. Cut a 6- by 10-inch rectangle from the joined fabric.

3. Spread a thin layer of glue on one side of the fabric. Wrap the fabric rectangle around the juice can so that the bottom edge of the fabric is flush with the bottom edge of the can; the fabric should extend slightly above the top edge of the can. Overlap the edges of the fabric to form the seam and press one edge flat over the other edge, as shown in Diagram 2.

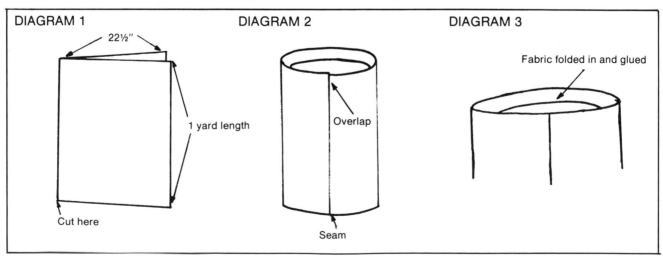

DIAGRAM 1

22½″

1 yard length

Cut here

DIAGRAM 2

Overlap

Seam

DIAGRAM 3

Fabric folded in and glued

4. Fold the top edge of the fabric to the inside of the can and glue it in place (Diagram 3).

5. Cut a piece of brown wrapping paper that is 4½ by 9 inches. Spread glue on one side of the paper and line the inside of the can with it.

6. Cut a piece of ribbon 9 inches long. Glue it around the can about ¾ inch down from the top and with the ends of the ribbon overlapping at the seam of the fabric (Diagram 4). This is the back of the pencil holder.

7. Cut a piece of ribbon 8 inches long. Tie it into a bow and glue the bow to the ribbon on the front of the can, as shown in the project photograph.

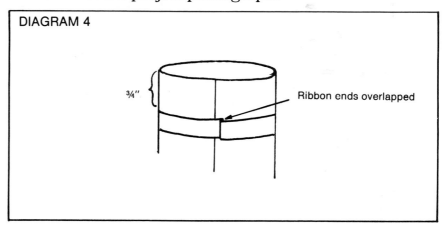

DIAGRAM 4

¾"

Ribbon ends overlapped

TELEPHONE BOOK

1. Cut two rectangles from the joined fabric, one that is 9½ by 14 inches and one that is 2¼ by 6¼ inches. Set the smaller piece aside.

2. Slide the directory pages out of the cover of your telephone book.

3. Spread a thin layer of glue on one side of the 9½- by 14-inch fabric rectangle. Center the cover of the telephone book right side down over the glue on the fabric and press the fabric and cover together; close the book while you are covering it with the fabric to be sure that you have allowed enough fabric around the binding to keep it flexible (Diagram 1).

4. Fold the top and bottom edges of the fabric to the inside of the cover, as shown in Diagram 2, and press down.

5. Fold the side edges to the inside of the cover and press down, making sure that the corners are folded neatly and flat (Diagram 3). Add an extra dot of glue at each corner if necessary.

6. Spread a thin layer of glue on one side of the 2¼- by 6¼-inch strip of joined fabric. Center the strip of fabric, glue side down, over the inside center fold of the cover, lining up one edge next to the slit in the cover but not covering the slit, as shown in Diagram 4, and press down.

7. Cut a piece of ribbon 9½ inches long. Following the project photograph for placement, glue the ribbon to the front of the cover, wrapping the ends over the top and bottom edges to the inside and gluing them down, as shown in Diagram 5.

8. Open the cover and glue the two pieces of heavy white paper to the inside of the cover, placing them so that all the edges of the fabric are hidden (Diagram 6). Slide the directory pages back into the cover.

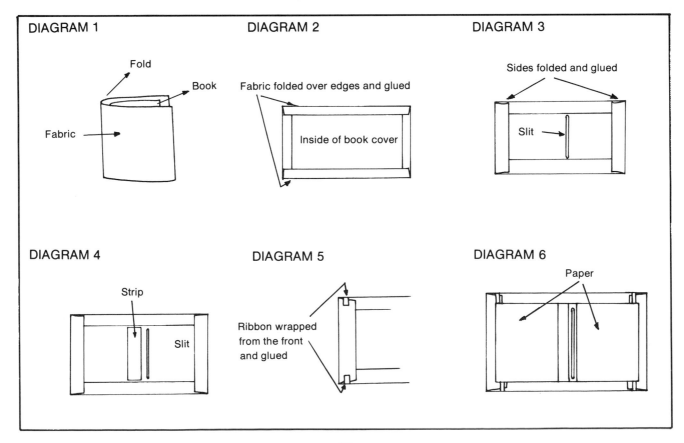

DIAGRAM 1

Fold

Book

Fabric

DIAGRAM 2

Fabric folded over edges and glued

Inside of book cover

DIAGRAM 3

Sides folded and glued

Slit

DIAGRAM 4

Strip

Slit

DIAGRAM 5

Ribbon wrapped from the front and glued

DIAGRAM 6

Paper

DESK BLOTTER

1. Cut two pieces from the joined fabric, each 4 by 15 inches.

2. Spread a layer of glue over one of the padded ends of the desk pad. Press one of the 4- by 15-inch pieces of joined fabric over it, centering the fabric so that there will be edges to turn under on all four sides. Repeat this procedure on the other end of the blotter. Make four 1-inch slits in the fabric at the points shown in Diagram 1.

3. Tuck the edges of the fabric under the padded end at the inner edges, as shown in Diagram 2.

4. Turn the blotter wrong side up. Fold the fabric over the top and bottom edges and glue it flat (Diagram 3).

5. Fold the fabric over the outside edges, making sure that the corners are folded neatly and flat, and glue it down (Diagram 4).

6. Cut two pieces of ribbon, each 15 inches long. Following the project photograph for placement, glue one piece on each end of the desk pad, wrapping the ends of the ribbon around to the back of the blotter and gluing them in place.

7. Cut a piece of brown wrapping paper 12 by 19 inches and glue it to the back of the blotter to cover the raw edges of the fabric and ribbon.

8. Cut a piece of blotter paper to fit the desk pad and insert it under the padded ends.

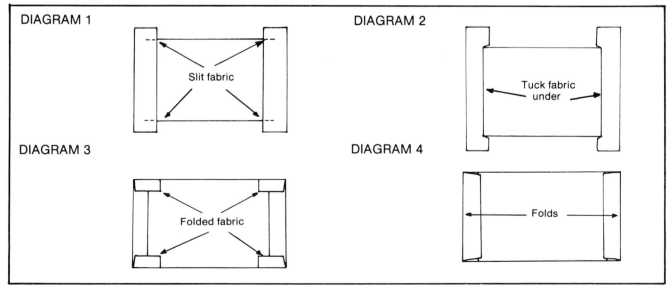

DIAGRAM 1 — Slit fabric

DIAGRAM 2 — Tuck fabric under

DIAGRAM 3 — Folded fabric

DIAGRAM 4 — Folds

6

COLONIAL LAP DESK

Our old-fashioned lap desk would make a handsome addition to any home—a perfect gift for Dad's birthday. We've made ours from scraps of plywood, and after it was stained and sealed with polyurethane, the grain produced an almost tortoise-shell finish. You could also make the desk from pine boards, but since most of them are cut a maximum of 12 inches wide, you would have to piece the wood together in order to get the 13½-inch width necessary.

MATERIALS

piece of plywood, 24 by 36 inches, exterior grade, or
  enough scraps to cut the seven pieces for the desk (see
  steps 1 and 2)
pencil
ruler
brown wrapping paper or other paper for cutting
  pattern
scissors
handsaw
wire brads, 1 inch long
hammer
wood stain, dark shade
cheesecloth
polyurethane, gloss finish
paintbrush, 1½ inches wide
steel wool, #000
sponge
turpentine
small amount of flat latex housepaint in colonial blue
screwdriver
one pair of decorative brass hinges and screws
one decorative brass drawer knob and plate
paste wax

PROCEDURE

1. With the pencil and ruler, mark rectangles on the
plywood to the following sizes:
  Back top piece: 4 by 13½ inches
  Top flap piece: 11½ by 13½ inches
  Back piece: 4 by 12⅞ inches
  Front piece: 2 by 12⅞ inches
  Bottom piece: 12 by 13½ inches

2. Using the brown wrapping paper, ruler, and pencil,
enlarge the pattern (see p. 13) for the side pieces and cut
it out.

3. Place the paper pattern on the plywood and trace
around it with the pencil. Remove the paper pattern and
cut the piece out of the plywood with the saw. Repeat
this procedure for the second side piece.

4. Following the list of measurements in step 1 to
identify each piece, begin nailing the pieces of the desk
together: Nail the two side pieces to the bottom piece, as
shown in Diagram 1.

PATTERN FOR SIDE PIECE

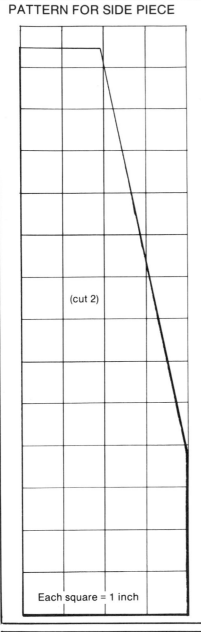

(cut 2)

Each square = 1 inch

5. Nail the back piece to the bottom and side edges (Diagram 2).

6. Nail the front piece to the bottom and vertical edges of the sides, as shown in Diagram 3.

7. Nail the back top piece to the back and back top edges of the sides (Diagram 4).

8. Stain the desk and the outside and side edges of the top flap by rubbing the stain into the wood with the cheesecloth. Allow the stain to dry according to manufacturer's directions.

9. Using the paintbrush, paint the outside and the edges with the polyurethane. Allow the polyurethane to dry, following manufacturer's directions.

10. Rub the desk and top flap with the steel wool. Remove the dust with a dampened sponge. Repeat steps 9 and 10.

11. Clean the paintbrush with the turpentine and then rinse it with soap and water.

12. Paint the inside of the desk and the inside of the top flap with the paintbrush and the blue housepaint, being careful not to let the paint run over the edges. If the paint does run, wipe it off immediately with a dampened sponge.

13. Following the project photograph for placement, use the screwdriver to attach the top flap to the top back piece of the desk with the hinges. Attach the brass knob and plate near the front of the flap in the center.

14. Give the desk a coat of paste wax, following manufacturer's directions.

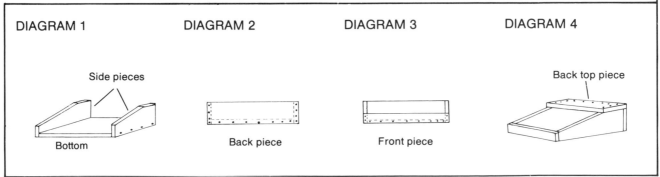

DIAGRAM 1

Side pieces

Bottom

DIAGRAM 2

Back piece

DIAGRAM 3

Front piece

DIAGRAM 4

Back top piece

2

AROUND THE HOUSE

PATCHWORK POINTS TABLE RUNNER

Our table runner, which is about 28 by 38 inches, will fit most standard-size rectangular tables nicely. It is also useful as a table setting for two if placed across the depth of the table. You might consider making a second one in Christmas colors for the holidays or in seasonal colors, such as rust and gold and browns for fall or in shades of pink and green for spring.

MATERIALS

piece of heavy cardboard, 3½ by 3½ inches
pencil or fabric marker
scraps of fabric in seven different colors and patterns
scissors
straight pins
needle
thread in colors to match fabrics
piece of fabric for backing, 30 by 40 inches

PROCEDURE

1. Using the cardboard square as a pattern, trace around it on the wrong side of the fabric, using the pencil or fabric marker (do not add seam allowance, since it has been figured into the 3½-inch square). Cut out the squares on the lines you have drawn. Keeping the squares in separate stacks according to fabric, cut the following:

30 squares of fabric No. 1
26 squares of fabric No. 2
22 squares of fabric No. 3
18 squares of fabric No. 4
14 squares of fabric No. 5
10 squares of fabric No. 6
4 squares of fabric No. 7

2. Arrange the squares as shown in Diagram 1. Note that the rows are on the diagonal.

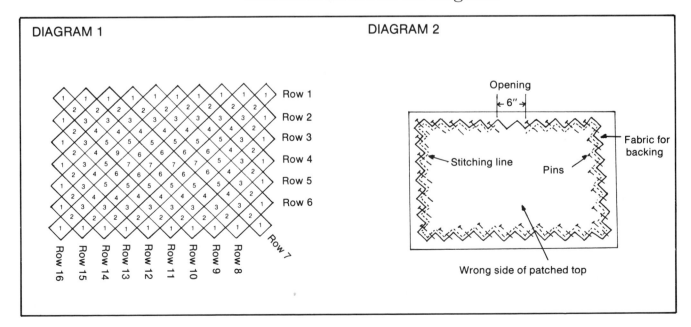

3. Using the needle and thread, begin sewing the fabric squares together at the edges with ¼-inch seam allowances and right sides facing. Start with the square at the upper right-hand corner. This square is Row 1 (see Diagram 1). Now pin the squares in Row 2 together, with a square of fabric No. 2 between two squares of fabric No. 1, as shown in Diagram 1. Stitch the squares together; remove the pins and press the seams flat. Pin Row 1 to Row 2. Stitch the rows together; remove the pins and press the seams flat. Reposition the rows as shown in Diagram 1. Referring to Diagram 1, continue pinning and stitching the squares and then the rows together until you have sewn all sixteen rows together.

4. Place the fabric for the backing right side up on a flat surface.

5. Center the patchwork you have just completed on top of the backing, right sides together. Pin the backing to the patchwork at each point. Stitch a ¼-inch seam around the points, leaving a 6-inch opening (Diagram 2).

6. Cut the backing into points, carefully following the points on the patchwork as a pattern (Diagram 3).

7. Clip each point to the seamline (Diagram 4).

8. Turn the runner right side out through the opening, slip stitch the opening closed, and press the piece.

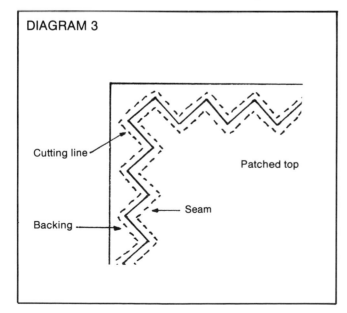

DIAGRAM 3

Cutting line

Patched top

Seam

Backing

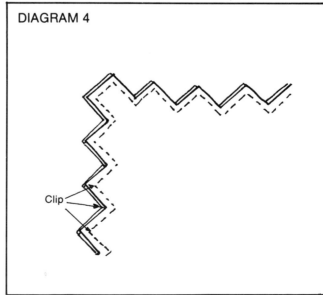

DIAGRAM 4

Clip

TULIP-PAINTED MIRROR

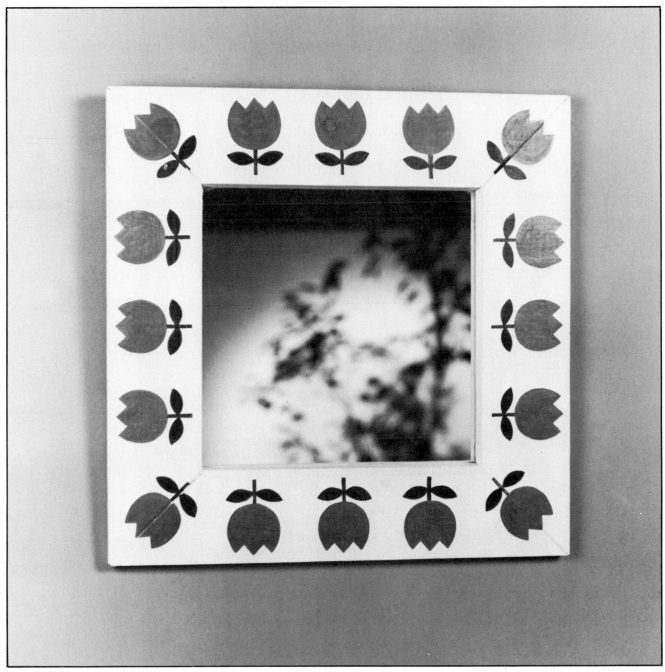

Plant this tulip-framed mirror in any room or hall for a cheerful note. Paint it in our bold red, white, and green combination or use your own color scheme. Ours is sized to fit the old mirror we wanted to reuse, but you can use one you already have and adjust the measurements if necessary, or have a mirror cut to fit. (A 12-by 12-inch piece of mirror should cost about three dollars.)

MATERIALS

yellow-pine board, 3⅜ inches wide by ¾ inch thick by 68
    inches long
ruler
pencil
handsaw
miter box
sandpaper, medium-grade for wood
masking tape
8 corrugated wood fasteners, each ⅜ inch
hammer
wood filler (optional)
semigloss latex paint in white
paintbrush, 1½ inches wide
piece of tracing paper for tracing pattern
scissors
piece of cardboard, 4 by 4 inches
fine paintbrush
acrylic paint in red and green
mirror, 12 by 12 inches
wire nails, ¾ inch long
square of brown wrapping paper, about 17 by 17 inches
white glue
picture hanger

PROCEDURE

1. Using the saw and the miter box, cut the pine board
into four pieces (see p. 13), making the outside
measurements of each piece 16¾ inches and the inside
measurements 10 inches, as shown in Diagram 1.

2. Lightly sand the four frame pieces you have just cut.
Place the smoothest side of each piece down on a flat,
firm surface. Put the pieces together in order to form the
frame of the mirror and tape the corners with the
masking tape to hold them in place (Diagram 2).

3. Join each corner of the frame with two wood
fasteners and remove the tape. Turn the frame right side
up. If necessary, fill the corners with the wood filler,
following the directions on the can. Allow the wood filler
to dry and sand the corners lightly.

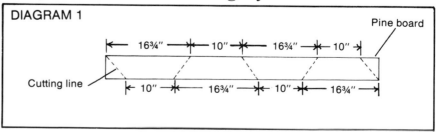

DIAGRAM 1

Pine board

|← 16¾" →|← 10" →|← 16¾" →|← 10" →|

Cutting line

|← 10" →|← 16¾" →|← 10" →|← 16¾" →|

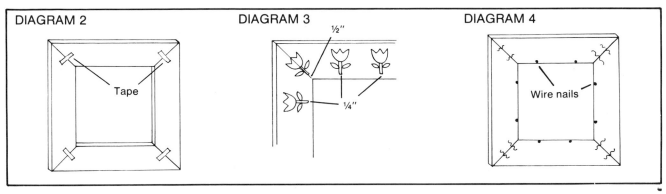

DIAGRAM 2

Tape

DIAGRAM 3

½"

¼"

DIAGRAM 4

Wire nails

FLOWER PATTERN

4. Paint the frame with two coats of the white latex paint, following the directions on the can. Allow the paint to dry.

5. Trace the flower pattern with the tracing paper and pencil. Cut the pattern out of the tracing paper and place it on the cardboard. Trace around the flower pattern again and cut it out of the cardboard.

6. Following the project photograph for placement of the flowers and placing the cardboard pattern on the frame so that the bottom of the stem is about ¼ inch from the inside edge of the frame along the sides and about ½ inch from the edge at the corners, trace around the cardboard sixteen times (Diagram 3).

7. Using the fine paintbrush, paint the tops of the flowers with the red paint and the stems and leaves with the green paint. Allow the paint to dry.

8. Turn the frame wrong side up. Place the mirror wrong side up on the frame so that it covers the opening in the center of the frame. Tap two of the wire nails into the wood on each side of the mirror at the edges of the mirror, as shown in Diagram 4. This will hold the mirror in place.

9. Tape the edges of the mirror to the frame with the masking tape to help secure it.

10. Cut a piece of brown paper exactly the size of the frame (about 16¾ by 16¾ inches). Glue the brown paper to the back of the mirror frame with the white glue.

11. Center the picture hanger on the top piece of the back of the frame and nail in place.

3

APPLIQUED POTHOLDERS

Here are three gay potholders, each bearing a very simple but effective appliquéd design, that will add country charm to any kitchen. Each made from scraps of fabric left over from other projects, they make welcome hostess gifts or Christmas presents for a special teacher. We give the directions in our color combinations, but we suggest you adapt the designs to use up your scraps.

MATERIALS

HEART
POTHOLDER

brown wrapping paper or other paper for cutting
    pattern
pencil
ruler
scissors
piece of heavy cardboard, about 6 by 6 inches
piece of fabric, 6 by 6 inches, in dark green and red print
tailor's chalk in white
needle
thread in colors to match fabrics
½ yard muslin
straight pins
¾ yard pin-dot fabric in red and white
2 pieces quilt batting, each 9¼ by 9¼ inches
quilting thread in dark green and white
quilting needle
plastic ring, about ¾ inch in diameter (optional)

PROCEDURE

1. Enlarge the pattern for the heart shape (see p. 13), using the brown wrapping paper, pencil, and ruler; cut it out.

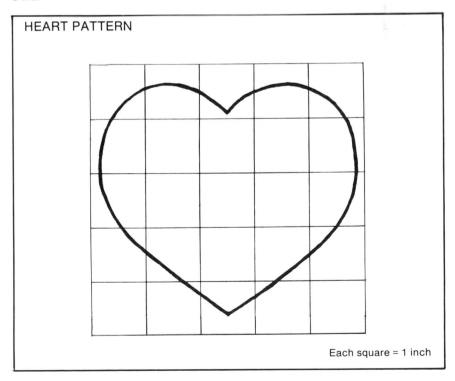

HEART PATTERN

Each square = 1 inch

2. Place the pattern on top of the cardboard and trace around it with the pencil. Remove the paper pattern and cut the heart shape out of the cardboard. This is the pattern for the heart-shaped appliqué.

3. Place the dark green and red fabric for the heart appliqué right side up on a flat surface. Lay the pattern on top of the fabric and trace around it with the tailor's chalk. Cut the heart out of the fabric, adding ¼ inch all around for a seam allowance.

4. Fold the raw edges of the appliqué back ¼ inch to the wrong side of the fabric (along the chalk line) and baste them in place.

5. Cut a square of muslin 6¼ by 6¼ inches. Pin the heart-shaped appliqué to the center of it with the right side of the fabric facing up. Baste the heart in place and remove the pins. Appliqué (see p. 11) the heart shape to the muslin and remove the basting.

6. Cut two strips of the red pin-dot fabric for the borders, each 2 by 9¼ inches, and two more that are 2 by 6¼ inches each.

7. With right sides of the fabric facing, pin the two strips that are 2 by 6¼ inches to opposite edges of the muslin square, as shown in Diagram 1.

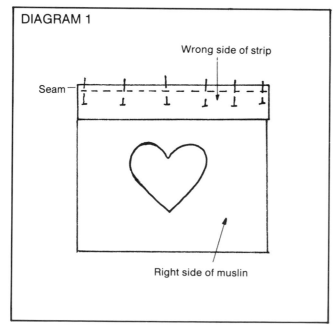

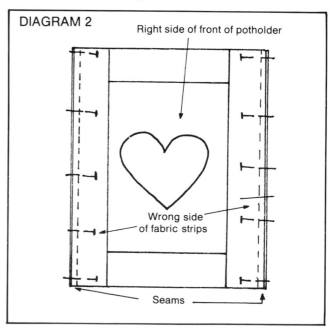

Stitch the strips to the muslin with a ¼-inch seam and remove the pins. Press the seams flat.

8. Using the method in step 7, sew the two 2- by 9¼-inch strips of fabric to the remaining two edges of the muslin (Diagram 2). This is the front of the potholder.

9. Cut another square of muslin that is 9¼ by 9¼ inches and place it on a flat surface. Lay one of the pieces of batting on top of it. Place the potholder front on top of the batting with the right side facing up. Working diagonally from the center out to the edges in eight directions, pin the three layers together and then baste them together, as shown in Diagram 3. Remove the pins.

10. With the quilting needle and dark green quilting thread, quilt around the heart-shaped appliqué (see p. 14) ¼ inch outside the shape on the muslin. Then quilt a line around the muslin square about ¼ inch in from the borders (Diagram 4). Remove the basting.

11. Cut a square of the pin-dot fabric for the backing that is 9¼ by 9¼ inches and place it on a flat surface right side up. Center the pattern for the heart appliqué on it and trace around it with the tailor's chalk.

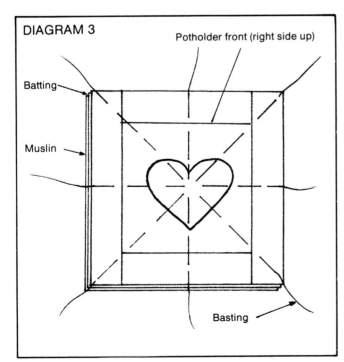

DIAGRAM 3

Potholder front (right side up)

Batting

Muslin

Basting

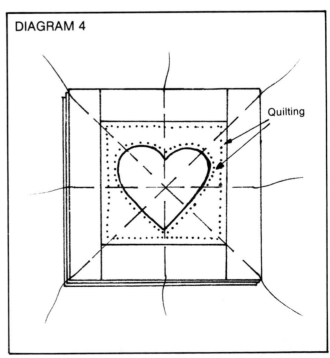

DIAGRAM 4

Quilting

12. Cut a square of the muslin 9¼ by 9¼ inches. Place the remaining piece of batting on top of the muslin and lay the pin-dot fabric with the heart tracing right side up on top. Working diagonally from the center out to the edges in eight directions, pin the three layers together (Diagram 5). Baste them together along the pin lines and remove the pins.

13. Quilt around the heart-shaped tracing with the white quilting thread and quilting needle, making one line ¼ inch inside the heart and another ¼ inch outside. Remove the basting. This is the back of the potholder.

14. Trim the batting and muslin back ½ inch on all four edges of the front and back pieces of the potholder (Diagram 6).

15. Pin the front and back pieces together around the four edges with the right sides facing. Baste them together and remove the pins. Sew them together with a ¼-inch seam allowance, leaving a 3-inch opening on one side (Diagram 7). Remove the basting.

16. Turn the potholder right side out through the opening and slip stitch the opening closed.

17. Sew the plastic ring to the top of the potholder or make a loop from the red and white pin-dot fabric and sew it to the top of the potholder in the center.

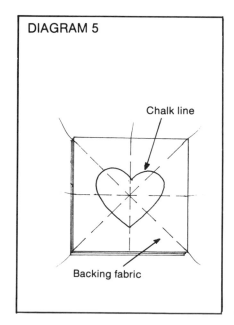

DIAGRAM 5

Chalk line

Backing fabric

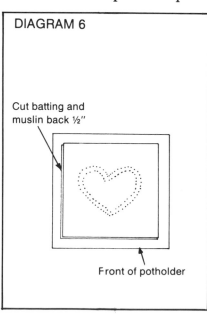

DIAGRAM 6

Cut batting and muslin back ½"

Front of potholder

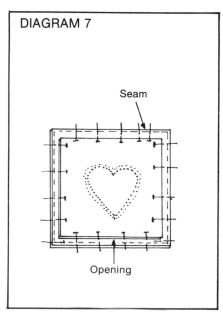

DIAGRAM 7

Seam

Opening

MATERIALS

WHALE POTHOLDER

brown wrapping paper or other paper for cutting
   pattern
pencil
ruler
scissors
piece of heavy cardboard, about 4½ by 7 inches
¼ yard muslin
needle
thread in color to match fabric
¼ yard calico fabric, in blue and white
straight pins
2 pieces quilt batting, each 8 by 8 inches
quilting thread in white and dark blue
quilting needle
embroidery needle
small amounts embroidery floss in yellow and black
tailor's chalk in white
plastic ring, about ¾ inch in diameter (optional)

PROCEDURE

1. Enlarge the pattern (see p. 13) for the whale appliqué, using the brown wrapping paper, pencil, and ruler; cut it out.

2. Place the pattern on top of the cardboard and trace around it with the pencil. Remove the pattern and cut the pattern out of the cardboard. This is the pattern for the muslin whale appliqué.

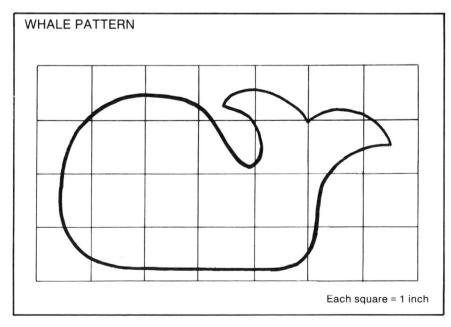

WHALE PATTERN

Each square = 1 inch

53

3. Cut a piece of muslin 4½ by 7 inches. Place the cardboard pattern on top of it and trace around it with the pencil. Cut the whale appliqué out of the muslin, cutting ¼ inch outside the tracing line all the way around to allow for the seam, as shown in Diagram 1.

4. Fold the raw edges back ¼ inch to the wrong side of the fabric (along the pencil line) and baste them in place.

5. Cut a square of the blue and white fabric 8 by 8 inches. Following the project photograph for placement, pin the whale appliqué diagonally to the right side of the fabric square. Baste the whale in place, remove the pins, and appliqué (see p. 11) around the whale. Remove the basting. This is now the top of the potholder.

6. Cut a square of muslin 8 by 8 inches. Place one of the squares of batting on top of the muslin and then lay the potholder top, right side up, on top of the batting.

7. Working diagonally from the center out to the edges in eight directions, pin the three layers together. Baste the three layers together along the pin lines and remove the pins (Diagram 2).

8. With the white quilting thread and the quilting needle, quilt (see p. 14) around the appliquéd whale about ¼ inch outside the edge, as shown in Diagram 3.

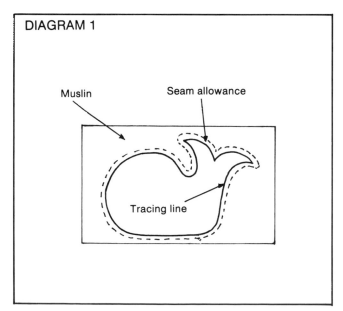

DIAGRAM 1

Muslin

Seam allowance

Tracing line

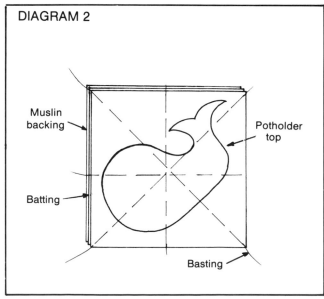

DIAGRAM 2

Muslin backing

Potholder top

Batting

Basting

9. With the dark blue quilting thread, quilt a line about ¼ inch inside the edge of the whale (Diagram 3). Remove the basting.

10. Following the project photograph for placement, draw a circle ¼ inch in diameter for the whale's eye with the pencil. Embroider the eye in the satin stitch (see p. 12) with the black embroidery floss.

11. Following the project photograph, draw the water spray with the white tailor's chalk. Embroider the water spray in the outline stitch (see p. 12) with the yellow embroidery floss.

12. Cut a piece of blue and white fabric 8 by 8 inches for the back of the potholder. Place it on a flat surface right side up. Center the cardboard whale pattern on it and trace around it with the white tailor's chalk.

13. Cut a piece of muslin 8 by 8 inches. Place the remaining piece of batting on top of the muslin and then lay the blue and white fabric right side up on top of the batting. Working diagonally from the center out to the edges in eight directions, pin the three layers together and then baste along the pin lines. Remove the pins.

14. With the white quilting thread and the quilting needle, quilt around the tracing of the whale pattern.

15. Being careful not to cut the blue and white fabric, trim the batting and muslin back ½ inch all around the four edges of both the back and front pieces of the potholder (Diagram 4).

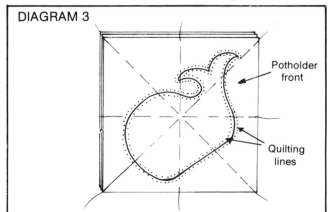

DIAGRAM 3

Potholder front

Quilting lines

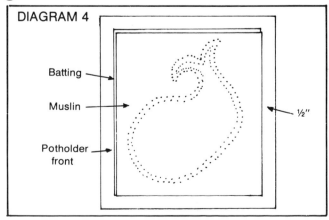

DIAGRAM 4

Batting

Muslin

Potholder front

½"

16. Cut two strips of blue and white fabric that are each 2 by 8½ inches and two more that are 2 by 9½ inches.

17. Wrong sides facing, fold one of the 2- by 8½-inch strips in half lengthwise. With right sides facing, pin the two long edges of the strip to one of the edges of the potholder front, as shown in Diagram 5. Repeat this step with the other 2- by 8½-inch strip on the opposite edge of the potholder.

18. Sew the strips to the edges of the potholder with a ¼-inch seam allowance and remove the pins.

19. Place the potholder front and the potholder back together with the right sides facing out and pin them together. Fold the folded edges of the strips you have sewn to the edges around to the back of the potholder to finish two of the raw edges of the potholder. Slip stitch the folded edges in place on the back, as shown in Diagram 6.

20. Fold the short ends of one of the 2- by 9½-inch strips in ½ inch to the wrong side of the fabric. Fold the strip in half lengthwise with wrong sides facing, as shown in Diagram 7.

21. Pin the two edges of the strip to one of the remaining raw edges on the potholder front. Stitch the strip to the potholder front with a ¼-inch seam. Repeat steps 20 and 21 with the last strip of fabric.

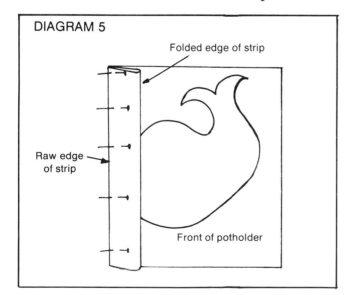

DIAGRAM 5

Folded edge of strip

Raw edge of strip

Front of potholder

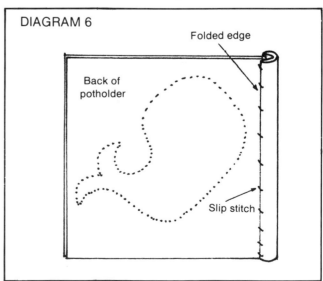

DIAGRAM 6

Folded edge

Back of potholder

Slip stitch

22. Fold the edges of the strips around to the back of the potholder and slip stitch them in place. Making sure that the raw edges are tucked in at the ends, slip stitch the four ends to finish the potholder (Diagram 8).

23. Sew the plastic ring to the top corner of the potholder, or make a loop from the calico fabric and sew it to the top corner.

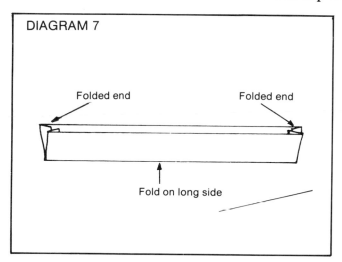

DIAGRAM 7

Folded end

Folded end

Fold on long side

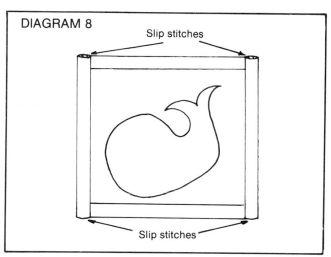

DIAGRAM 8

Slip stitches

Slip stitches

MATERIALS

CALICO TULIP POTHOLDER

brown wrapping paper or other paper for cutting pattern
pencil
ruler
scissors
piece of heavy cardboard, about 5 by 6 inches
piece of fabric, 4 by 4 inches, in a multicolored print on a dark blue background
tailor's chalk in white
¼ yard pin-dot fabric in kelly green and white
needle
thread in colors to match fabrics
¼ yard muslin
straight pins
2 pieces quilt batting, each 8¾ by 9½ inches
quilting thread in dark blue and white
quilting needle
plastic ring, about ¾ inch in diameter (optional)

PROCEDURE

1. Enlarge the patterns (see p. 13) for the flower, stem, and leaf, using the brown wrapping paper, pencil, and ruler; cut them out.

2. Place the pattern pieces on top of the cardboard and trace around them with the pencil. Remove the paper patterns and cut the shapes out of the cardboard. These will be your patterns for the appliqués.

3. Place the dark blue square of fabric right side up and place the pattern for the flower appliqué on top of it. Trace around the pattern with the tailor's chalk. Cut the flower shape out of the fabric, cutting ¼ inch outside the line all the way around to allow for the seam (Diagram 1).

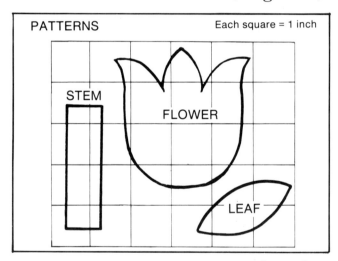

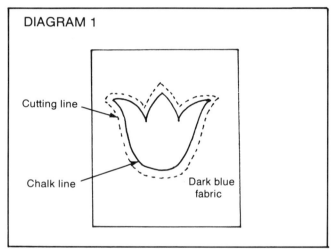

4. Place the pattern for the stem and leaf on the right side of a piece of the green pin-dot fabric. Trace around them with the tailor's chalk and cut them out, adding ¼ inch all around for a seam allowance. Cut a second leaf in the same way.

5. Fold the raw edges on all the appliqué pieces back ¼ inch to the wrong side of the fabric (along the chalk lines) and baste them in place.

6. Cut a piece of muslin 6 by 6¾ inches. Following the project photograph for placement, pin the stem, leaves, and flower in place on the muslin. The bottom edge of the flower should overlap the top edge of the stem slightly and the stem should overlap the inner edge of the leaves. Baste the pieces in place and remove the pins. Appliqué the pieces (see p. 11) to the muslin and remove the basting.

7. Cut two strips of the green pin-dot fabric, each 2 by 6¾ inches, and two more that are 1¾ by 8¾ inches.

8. With right sides of the fabric facing, pin the two strips that are 6¾ inches long to the two 6¾-inch sides of the muslin, as shown in Diagram 2.

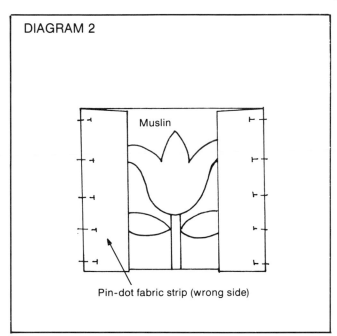

DIAGRAM 2

Muslin

Pin-dot fabric strip (wrong side)

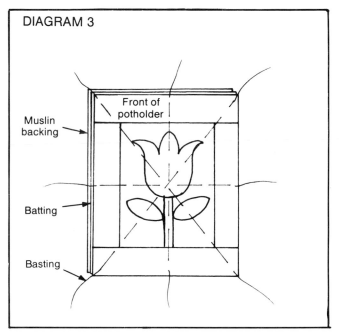

DIAGRAM 3

Front of potholder

Muslin backing

Batting

Basting

9. Stitch the strips to the muslin with a ¼-inch seam. Remove the pins and press the seams flat.

10. Pin the remaining two strips of fabric to the top and bottom edges of the muslin with the right sides of the fabric facing. Stitch them in place with ¼-inch seams. Remove the pins and press the seams flat. This is the front of the potholder.

11. Cut a piece of muslin 8¾ by 9½ inches and place it on a flat surface. Place one of the pieces of batting on top of it, and then lay the potholder top, right side up, on top of the batting. Working from the center out to the edges in eight directions, pin all three layers together and then baste them together, as shown in Diagram 3; remove the pins.

12. With the dark blue quilting thread and the quilting needle, quilt (see p. 14) a line around the flower, stem, and leaf appliqués about ¼ inch out from the edge of the appliqués.

13. Cut a piece of green pin-dot fabric 8¾ by 9½ inches. Place it on a flat surface, right side up. Center the pattern for the flower appliqué on it and trace around it with the tailor's chalk.

14. Cut a piece of muslin 8¾ by 9½ inches. Place the remaining piece of batting on top of the muslin. Place the green pin-dot fabric with the flower tracing, right side up, on top of the batting. Working from the center out to the edges in eight directions, pin the three layers together. Baste them together along the pin lines and remove the pins.

15. Quilt around the flower tracing with the white quilting thread and the quilting needle. Remove the basting. This is the back of the potholder.

16. Trim the muslin and batting back ½ inch around all four edges of the front and back pieces of the potholder (Diagram 4).

17. With right sides facing, pin the front and back pieces together around the four edges. Stitch the pieces together with a ¼-inch seam, leaving a 3-inch opening on one side.

18. Remove the pins and turn the potholder right side out through the opening. Slip stitch the opening closed.

19. Sew the plastic ring to the top of the potholder or make a loop from the green pin-dot fabric and sew it to the top of the potholder near the center.

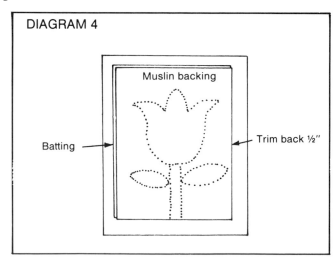

DIAGRAM 4

Muslin backing

Batting

Trim back ½"

QUILTED TEA COZY AND POTHOLDER

You will be amazed at how long the tea stays warm when you use a tea cozy. A great source of fabric for this charming, "countrified" project is an old quilted bathrobe or bed cover, or even, perhaps a set of quilted placemats. For a smashing table setting, you might coordinate the fabric with the fabric used in the Patchwork Christmas Tablecloth project or the Patchwork Points Table Runner.

MATERIALS

brown wrapping paper or other paper for cutting
 pattern
pencil
ruler
scissors
about 1 square yard prequilted fabric
straight pins
needle
thread in color to match fabric
1¼ yards pregathered eyelet lace, about 1 inch wide, in
 white

PROCEDURE

1. Using the brown wrapping paper, pencil, and ruler, enlarge the pattern pieces (see p. 13) for the cozy and cut them out.

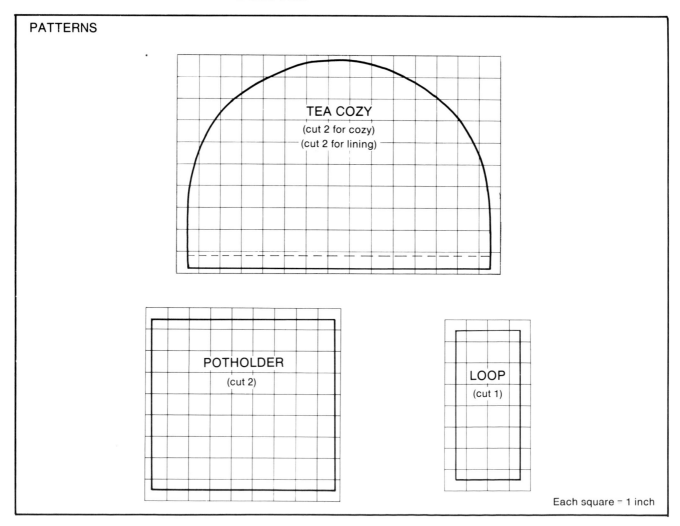

PATTERNS

TEA COZY
(cut 2 for cozy)
(cut 2 for lining)

POTHOLDER
(cut 2)

LOOP
(cut 1)

Each square ‒ 1 inch

2. Fold the fabric in half and pin the pattern pieces to it, following Diagram 1.

Following the pattern pieces, cut the fabric pieces out, cutting along the dotted line for the two lining pieces.

3. Pin the lining pieces together with the right sides of the fabric facing. Sew a ½-inch seam around the curve of the pieces, as shown in Diagram 2; set aside.

4. Pin the straight edge of the eyelet lace to the right side of the fabric along the curved edge of one of the outside pieces of the cozy, as shown in Diagram 3.

Baste the lace in place and remove the pins.

5. Lay the strip of fabric out for the loop wrong side up and fold into thirds lengthwise, as shown in Diagram 4. Press the strip along the folds. Turn the raw edge under ½ inch and slip stitch closed (Diagram 4A).

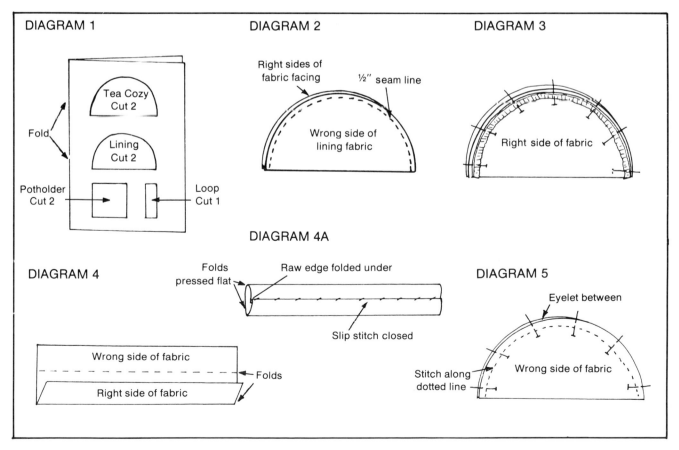

DIAGRAM 1

Fold

Tea Cozy
Cut 2

Lining
Cut 2

Potholder
Cut 2

Loop
Cut 1

DIAGRAM 2

Right sides of fabric facing

½" seam line

Wrong side of lining fabric

DIAGRAM 3

Right side of fabric

DIAGRAM 4A

Folds pressed flat

Raw edge folded under

Slip stitch closed

DIAGRAM 4

Wrong side of fabric

Folds

Right side of fabric

DIAGRAM 5

Eyelet between

Stitch along dotted line

Wrong side of fabric

6. With the seam facing out, sew one end of the fabric strip to the center of the right side of the cozy piece with the lace edging. Bring the other end of the strip around to meet the first, forming a loop, and sew it in place.

7. Lay the second outside piece for the cozy on top of the first one with right sides facing. Pin the curved edges together (Diagram 5). Baste along the curved edge, leaving a ¼-inch seam allowance. Remove the pins and stitch along the basted line. Remove the basting and turn the cozy right side out.

8. Slide the lining you sewed earlier into the outer portion of the cozy and line up the bottom edges. Turn the raw edges along the bottom in so that they are hidden between the outside of the cozy and the lining (Diagram 6). Slip stitch the bottom edge closed.

9. Using one of the pieces of fabric cut for the potholder, pin the straight edge of the lace along two opposing right-side edges. Fold the ends of the eyelet under twice to conceal the raw ends. Baste the eyelet in place and remove the pins (Diagram 7).

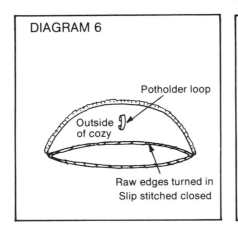

DIAGRAM 6

Potholder loop

Outside of cozy

Raw edges turned in
Slip stitched closed

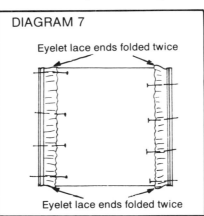

DIAGRAM 7

Eyelet lace ends folded twice

Eyelet lace ends folded twice

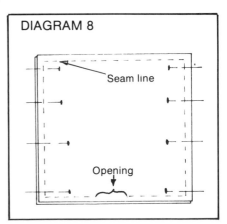

DIAGRAM 8

Seam line

Opening

10. Place the second piece of fabric for the potholder on top of the first with right sides of the fabric facing. Sew around the outside edge with a ½-inch seam allowance, leaving a 2-inch opening on one edge (Diagram 8).

Turn the potholder right side out through the opening and slip stitch the opening closed.

11. Slide the potholder into the loop, as shown in the project photograph.

EIGHT-POINTED STAR PILLOW

This pillow, which can be made in many variations, will be the star of any room. We have used three fabrics to make the star, but it can be made with one or two. This pattern can be carried out into a beautiful quilt if you are ambitious, and it is a fun way to turn scraps of fabric into a pretty and useful object.

MATERIALS

piece of tracing paper for tracing pattern
pencil
ruler
scissors
piece of cardboard, 2 by 5 inches
three different colors and/or patterns of cotton fabrics
fabric marker (optional)
straight pins
thread in colors to match fabrics
needle
square of muslin, 17 by 17 inches
square of muslin for backing when you quilt, 16½ by
    16½ inches
square of quilt batting, 17 by 17 inches
quilting thread in the color of your choice
quilting needle
square of fabric for back of pillow, 16½ by 16½ inches
1 pound of polyester stuffing

PROCEDURE

1. Place the tracing paper over the pattern for the diamond-shaped patch and trace over it, using the pencil and ruler. Cut the pattern out of the tracing paper and place it on top of the cardboard. Carefully trace around it and cut the pattern out of the cardboard. This is the actual size of the fabric pieces you will cut; do not add seam allowances.

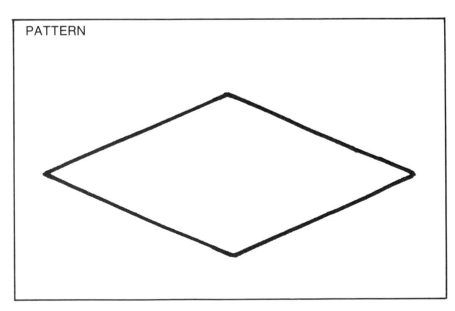

PATTERN

2. Place the cardboard pattern on the wrong side of one of the pieces of fabric. Trace around it with the fabric marker or pencil. Cut the fabric along the lines you have just drawn. Repeat this procedure until you have cut out eight patches of fabric No. 1, sixteen patches of fabric No. 2, and eight patches of fabric No. 3 (Diagram 1). Following Diagram 1 for placement, lay the diamond-shaped pieces, right sides up, on a flat surface.

DIAGRAM 1

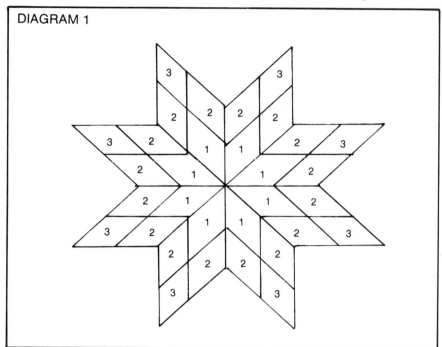

DIAGRAM 2

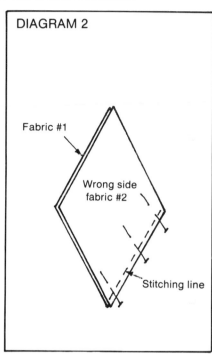

Fabric #1

Wrong side fabric #2

Stitching line

3. With right sides of the fabric facing, pin a patch of fabric No. 1 to a piece of fabric No. 2 along the edges that adjoin, as shown in Diagram 2. Baste along the edge, leaving a ¼-inch seam allowance; remove the pins. Stitch along the basting line. Remove the basting, spread the patches open, and press the seam flat.

4. Following the instructions in step 3, sew a patch of fabric No. 2 to a patch of fabric No. 3. With right sides facing, pin the first two pieces you stitched together to the second two along the long edge, as shown in Diagram 3. Stitch them together, leaving a ¼-inch seam allowance, and remove the pins. Open the sections and press the seams flat.

5. Repeat steps 3 and 4 with the remaining patches cut from the three fabrics to make the seven remaining points of the star.

6. With right sides of the fabric facing, pin two of the points together along one edge (Diagram 4). Stitch them together, leaving a ¼-inch seam allowance; remove the pins. Open the sections and press the seam flat.

7. Following the instructions in step 6, sew a third section to the edge of the two you have just sewn (Diagram 5).

8. Sew the fourth section to the third section, as shown in Diagram 6. The four sections you have just sewn together make up one half of the star. Set this half aside and, following the instructions in steps 6, 7, and 8, sew the remaining four sections together.

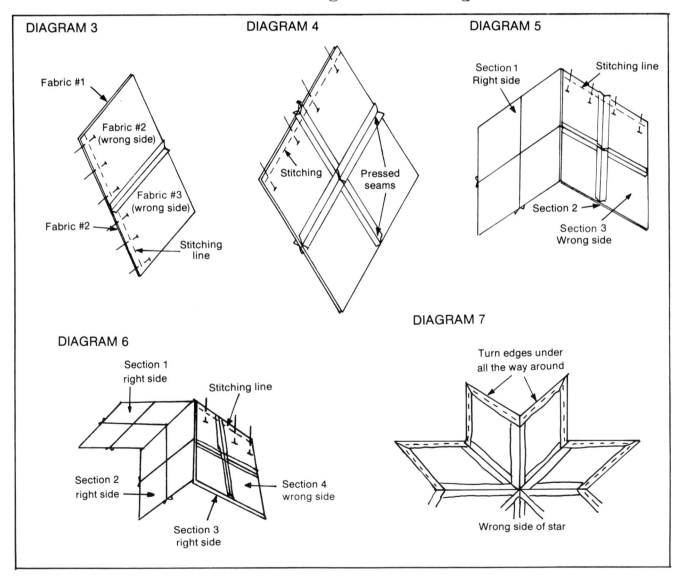

DIAGRAM 3

Fabric #1

Fabric #2 (wrong side)

Fabric #3 (wrong side)

Fabric #2

Stitching line

DIAGRAM 4

Stitching

Pressed seams

DIAGRAM 5

Section 1 Right side

Stitching line

Section 2

Section 3 Wrong side

DIAGRAM 7

Turn edges under all the way around

Wrong side of star

DIAGRAM 6

Section 1 right side

Stitching line

Section 2 right side

Section 4 wrong side

Section 3 right side

9. With the right sides facing, pin the two halves of the star together along the straight edge. Baste a ¼-inch seam and remove the pins. Stitch the seam and remove the basting. Open the star and press the seam flat.

10. Turn the raw edges under ¼ inch along the outer edges of the star and baste them in place (Diagram 7).

11. Place the star, right side up, in the center of the 14-inch square of muslin. Pin it in place and then baste it to the muslin. Remove the pins. Appliqué (see p. 11) the star to the muslin and remove the basting.

12. Cut four strips of fabric No. 3, each 2 by 14 inches long. Cut four squares of fabric No. 1, each 2 by 2 inches.

13. With right sides facing, pin, baste, and sew two of the 14-inch-long strips to opposite edges of the muslin square with a ¼-inch seam, as shown in Diagram 8. Press the seams flat.

14. With right sides facing and with a ¼-inch seam allowance, sew the four 2- by 2-inch squares of fabric No. 1 to opposite ends of the two remaining strips of fabric No. 3 , as shown in Diagram 9. Press the seams flat.

15. With right sides facing, pin the two strips with the squares sewn to the ends to the two remaining edges of the muslin square, as shown in Diagram 10. Sew the strips to the muslin with ¼-inch seams. Press the seams flat.

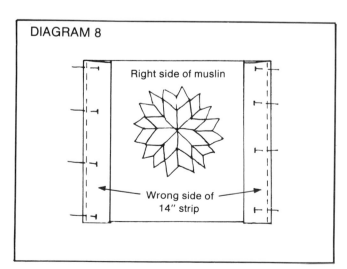

DIAGRAM 8

Right side of muslin

Wrong side of 14" strip

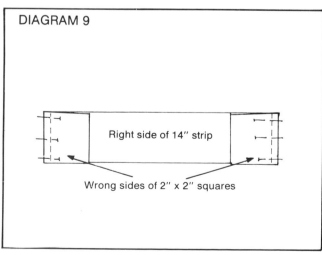

DIAGRAM 9

Right side of 14" strip

Wrong sides of 2" x 2" squares

16. Following the project photograph, draw a line, using a pencil or the fabric marker, on the muslin ¼ inch outside the star shape all around. Draw another line ¼ inch inside the fabric borders on all four edges of the pillow.

17. Place the 17-inch square of muslin on a flat surface. Place the square of batting on top of it. Place the pillow top with the star on it, right side up, on top of the batting (Diagram 11).

18. Starting from the center and working out to the edges, pin the three layers together and baste along the pin lines, as shown in Diagram 11. Remove the pins.

19. Using the quilting thread and quilting needle, quilt (see p. 14) the three layers together along the lines you have drawn on the muslin.

20. Place the quilted pillow top wrong side up. Being careful not to cut the pillow front, trim the batting and the muslin backing about ½ inch in on all four sides, as shown in Diagram 12.

21. Turn the quilted pillow top right side up. With right sides facing, place the square of fabric for the pillow back on top of it and pin them together along the edges. Baste them along all four sides and remove the pins. Stitch a ¼-inch seam all around the pillow, leaving a 3-inch opening on one edge. Remove the basting and turn the pillow right side out through the opening.

22. Stuff the pillow with the polyester stuffing and slip stitch the 3-inch opening closed.

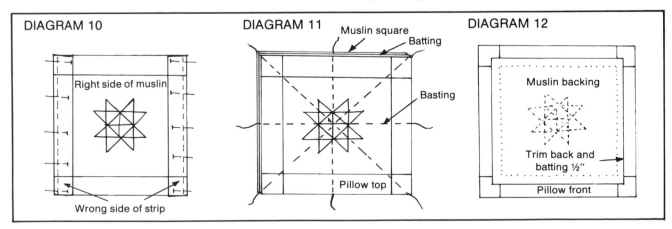

DIAGRAM 10

Right side of muslin

Wrong side of strip

DIAGRAM 11

Muslin square

Batting

Basting

Pillow top

DIAGRAM 12

Muslin backing

Trim back and batting ½"

Pillow front

6

DRESDEN PLATE PILLOW

The design on this pillow is a traditional American quilt pattern. It is an ideal way to use up fabric scraps, since each patch that goes into making up the "plate" is small, even though the finished pillow is a generous 17-inch square. If you are really ambitious, you may want to make a whole quilt from this pattern.

MATERIALS

tracing paper for tracing pattern
pencil
ruler
scissors
piece of cardboard, 3 by 5 inches
scraps of cotton fabric in several different colors and
    patterns
fabric marker (optional)
straight pins
needle
thread in colors to match fabrics
square of muslin, 14 by 14 inches
¼ yard fabric, 45 inches wide, in dark blue, for borders
square of muslin, 18 by 18 inches, for backing (when
    quilting)
square of batting, 18 by 18 inches
quilting thread in rust
quilting needle
square of fabric, 18 by 18 inches, in rust, for back of
    pillow
1 pound of polyester stuffing

PROCEDURE

1. Place the tracing paper over the pattern for the patch
and trace over it, using the pencil and the ruler. Cut the
patch pattern out of the tracing paper and place it on
top of the cardboard. Carefully trace around it and cut
the pattern out of the cardboard. This is the actual size
of the fabric pieces you will cut; do not add seam
allowances.

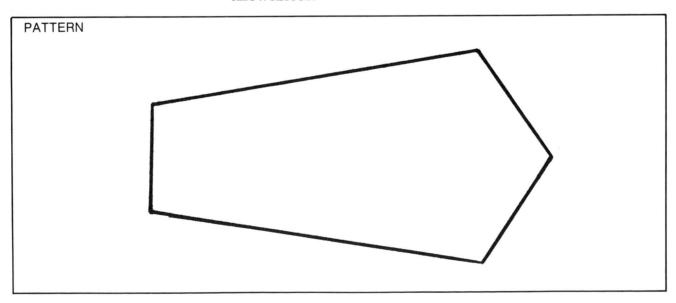

PATTERN

2. Place the cardboard pattern on the wrong side of one of the fabric scraps. Trace around it with the fabric marker or the pencil. Cut the fabric along the lines you have just drawn. Repeat this procedure twenty more times, using the other fabric scraps. If you want, you can use each fabric more than once, but be sure to use a variety of fabrics.

3. Using the project photograph as a guide, arrange the patches in a circle. Adjust them until the colors are in a pleasing arrangement. Select two patches of the "plate" that you have placed side by side and place them together with the right sides of the fabric facing; pin them together along one side. Using the thread and needle, stitch them together with a ¼-inch seam allowance (Diagram 1). Remove the pins.

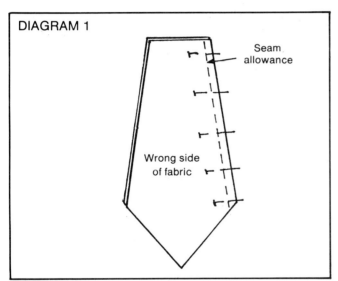

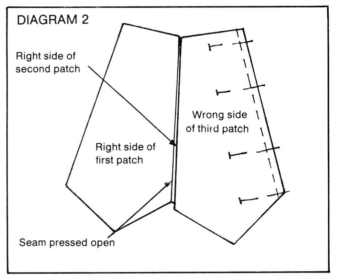

4. Open the patches with the wrong side facing up and spread them flat. Press the seam flat. With right sides facing, pin the third patch to the second along one side. Stitch the seam with a ¼-inch seam allowance and remove the pins. Press the seam flat (Diagram 2).

5. Repeat this process until you have joined all twenty-one of the patches and you have formed a complete circle.

6. Turn the raw edges around the center circle of the "plate" to the wrong side ¼ inch and baste them flat. Repeat this procedure with the raw edges of the points of the "plate" around the outside.

7. Lay the 14-inch square of muslin on a flat surface and place the "plate" right side up in the center of it. Pin the "plate" in place. Baste around the outer edge and around the inner circle. Remove the pins. Appliqué (see p. 11) the "plate" to the muslin. Remove the basting.

8. Cut four strips of the dark blue fabric for borders, cutting two 2¼- by 14-inch strips and two 2¼- by 18½-inch strips. With right sides together, pin one of the 14-inch strips to one edge of the muslin with the "plate" appliquéd to it, as shown in Diagram 3.

Baste the strip to the muslin along the edge and remove the pins. Stitch a ¼-inch seam along the edge and remove the basting. Press the seam flat. Repeat this step with the second 14-inch strip on the opposite edge of the muslin (Diagram 3).

9. Following the directions in step 8, sew the two 18½-inch strips along the other two edges of the muslin. This is the pillow top.

10. Using the fabric marker or a pencil, draw on the muslin one line ¼ inch inside the borders, one line ¼ inch inside the center circle of the "plate," and one line ¼ inch outside the outer pointed edge, as shown in Diagram 4. These will mark where to quilt later on.

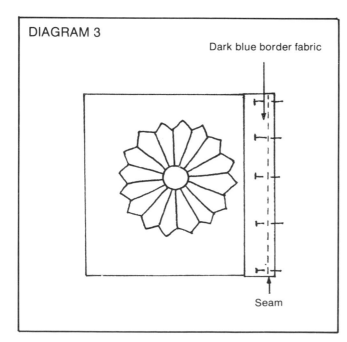

DIAGRAM 3

Dark blue border fabric

Seam

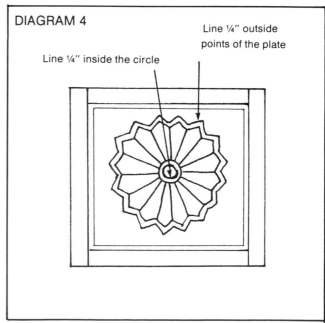

DIAGRAM 4

Line ¼" outside points of the plate

Line ¼" inside the circle

11. Place the 18-inch square of muslin on a flat surface. Place the 18-inch square of batting on top of it. Place the pillow top, right side up, on top of the batting (Diagram 5).

12. Starting from the center and working out to the edge, pin the three layers together and baste along the pin lines, as shown in Diagram 5. Remove the pins.

13. Using the rust-colored quilting thread and the quilting needle, quilt (see p. 14) the three layers together along the lines you have drawn on the muslin.

14. Turn the quilted pillow top wrong side up. Being careful not to cut the pillow front, trim the batting and the muslin backing about ½ inch on all four edges, as shown in Diagram 6.

15. Turn the quilted pillow top right side up. With right sides facing, place the 18-inch square of rust-colored fabric on top of it. Pin the pillow top to the rust-colored fabric and baste around all four edges. Remove the pins and stitch them together with a ¼-inch seam, leaving an opening 3 inches long on one side. Remove the basting. Turn the pillow right side out through the opening.

16. Stuff the pillow with the polyester stuffing and slip stitch the opening closed.

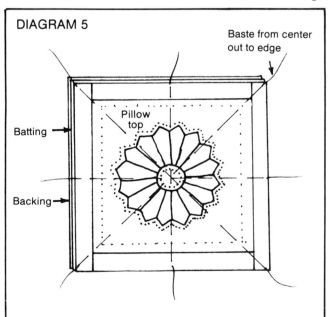

DIAGRAM 5

Baste from center out to edge

Pillow top

Batting

Backing

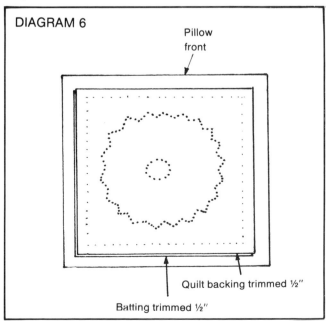

DIAGRAM 6

Pillow front

Quilt backing trimmed ½"

Batting trimmed ½"

7

STENCILED WELCOME SIGN

This stenciled sign is a charming, old-fashioned way to welcome people to your own home or it makes an ideal housewarming gift. We painted ours white and colonial blue, but you can gear yours to a specific color scheme. We made this from scrap lumber and molding, but it's equally effective without the molding, which eliminates several steps.

MATERIALS

handsaw
miter box
5 feet of corner guard molding, ¾ inch wide (optional)
piece of ¾-inch yellow-pine board, 12¼ by 15½ inches
ruler
hammer
wire nails, ¾ inch long
paintbrush, 1½ inches wide
small amount latex housepaint in white
brown wrapping paper or other paper for cutting
    pattern
pencil
scissors
two pieces cardboard, each 10¾ by 14½ inches
masking tape
two pieces stencil paper or acetate, each 10¾ by 14½
    inches
single-edged razor blade
acrylic paint in color of your choice
aluminum-foil pie plate or paper plate
sponge
newspaper
graphite paper or carbon paper
fine paintbrush
sawtooth picture hanger (optional)
clear polyurethane (optional)
nails (optional)
wood drill (optional)
wood screws (optional)

PROCEDURE

Note: If you are framing the board, start with step 1; if not, start with step 2.

1. Using the saw and the miter box (see p. 13), cut four pieces of molding to fit the measurements of each edge of the pine board. Place the pieces of molding that you have just cut around the board to form the frame. Attach the frame to the board by nailing it to the edges of the board; use three wire nails to attach each piece, placing one in the middle of the molding and one at each end, as shown in Diagram 1.

2. Using the 1½-inch-wide paintbrush and the white latex housepaint, paint the board and molding, following manufacturer's directions. Give the board at least two coats of paint, allowing it to dry between coats.

3. Using the brown wrapping paper, pencil, and ruler, enlarge the two stencil patterns (see p. 13) and cut them out of the paper.

4. Place the pattern for the house on one of the pieces of cardboard so that the chimneys are 1¼ inches from the top of the cardboard and the sides of the house are 1¼ inches from the sides; tape it in place (Diagram 2). Trace around the pattern and remove it from the cardboard.

5. Place one of the sheets of stencil paper or acetate on top of the cardboard so that the edges line up with the edges of the cardboard in order to center the house design properly. Use the ruler and the razor blade to cut along each line of the pattern with a single, neat line.

6. Following steps 4 and 5, use the remaining piece of cardboard and stencil paper to cut the stencil for the door and windows.

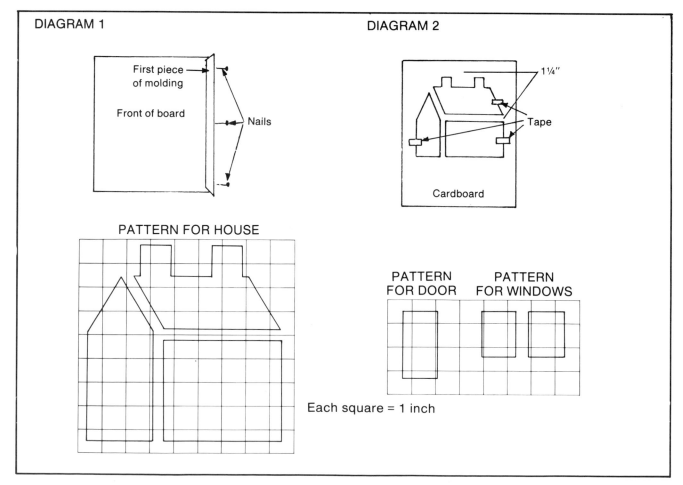

DIAGRAM 1

First piece of molding

Front of board

Nails

DIAGRAM 2

1¼"

Tape

Cardboard

PATTERN FOR HOUSE

PATTERN FOR DOOR   PATTERN FOR WINDOWS

Each square = 1 inch

7. Place the stencil for the house on the pine board 1¼ inches below the top and tape the edges of it to the board to prevent it from slipping.

8. Squeeze some of the acrylic paint onto the pie plate. Dip the sponge into the paint and remove the excess by dabbing the sponge onto the newspaper. Dab the paint into the cut-out areas of the stencil (see p. 15). Allow the paint to dry slightly, and carefully remove the stencil. Allow the paint to dry thoroughly.

9. Place the stencil for the door and windows on the board and tape the edges to the board. Follow the procedure in step 8 to stencil the door and windows with the white housepaint used to paint the board.

10. Using the brown wrapping paper, pencil, and ruler, enlarge the pattern (see p. 13) for the welcome sign. Place a piece of graphite or carbon paper face down on the board and tape it in place. Place the tracing on top about 1¼ inches below the house and tape the edges to the board (Diagram 3). Trace around the pattern with a pencil; remove the tracing and graphite or carbon paper.

11. Using the fine paintbrush and the acrylic paint, paint the letters and the heart shape.

12. If you are hanging the sign inside, nail a picture hanger to the back of the sign, near the top edge. If you are using the sign outside, give it two or three coats of the polyurethane to protect it from the weather. Nail the sign to the house or another surface, or drill a hole in the pine board at each of the four corners about ½ inch in from the molding, and use the wood screws to attach it.

PATTERN

Each square = 1 inch

DIAGRAM 3

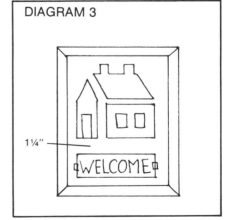

1¼"

CALICO HOUSE PORTRAIT

This project makes a wonderful personal gift and keepsake. Capture the personality of a friend's house and send it with the family as a moving-away gift or give it as a housewarming present. Or you might make yourself a picture of the house you grew up in. This makes a great family project when you create a portrait of your own house.

MATERIALS

color photograph of the house (see step 1)
tracing paper for tracing pattern
tape (masking or cellophane)
pencil
ruler
paper the size you wish your finished portrait to be
scissors
scraps of calico, gingham, and cotton fabrics
straight pins
fabric marker (optional)
needle
thread in colors to match fabrics
piece of fabric for the background, in light blue for a day
   sky or dark blue for night (this can be calico, checked,
   or solid, but it must be 2 inches larger all around
   than the finished portrait)
various shades of cotton embroidery floss
embroidery needle
bits of lace and trims
frame (optional)

PROCEDURE

1. Take a photograph of the house you have chosen to do a "portrait" of, standing directly in front of the house and facing the center of it to eliminate angles to help to simplify the shapes.

2. Place a piece of tracing paper over the photograph and tape it at the edges so that the paper will not shift.

3. Draw a grid of equal-sized boxes on the tracing paper over the picture so that the number of boxes across and down the grid equals the number of inches across and down you want the final portrait size to be. Example: Our finished portrait is 15 by 18 inches, so our grid has fifteen boxes down and eighteen boxes across. See Diagram 1.

4. Trace around the main shapes in the photograph, such as the house, large trees, a walkway, fence area, etc. Avoid too much detail—you can add it later with embroidery and trims.

5. Draw a rectangle on the sheet of paper the size you wish the final "portrait" to be. Draw a grid of 1-inch boxes on the paper. (If your portrait is going to be 15 by 20 inches, you will have fifteen boxes going down and twenty going across.) Following the instructions on page 13, enlarge the shapes you have traced on the small grid by drawing them on the large grid.

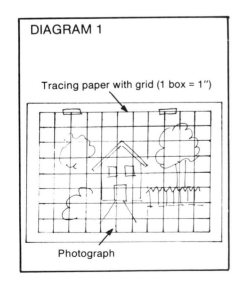

DIAGRAM 1

Tracing paper with grid (1 box = 1″)

Photograph

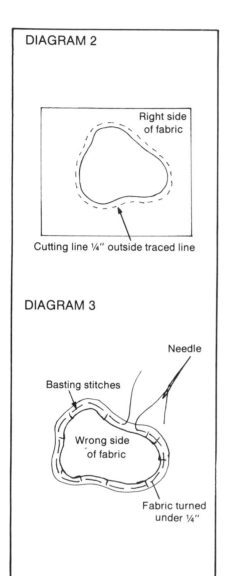

DIAGRAM 2

Right side
of fabric

Cutting line ¼″ outside traced line

DIAGRAM 3

Needle

Basting stitches

Wrong side
of fabric

Fabric turned
under ¼″

6. Cut around the shapes on the large grid to make patterns for the main parts of your picture.

7. Select appropriately-colored fabrics for the different pattern pieces—greens for trees, grass, and bushes, browns for tree trunks, and so on. Be sure to select carefully for the main body of the house, since this is the focal point of the picture.

8. Choose one pattern piece and pin it to the right side of the fabric you have selected for that piece. Trace around the pattern piece with the fabric marker or a pencil.

9. Remove the pins and cut around the shape ¼ inch outside the tracing line, as shown in Diagram 2.

Set this piece aside and repeat steps 8 and 9 with the rest of the pattern pieces.

10. Select one fabric picture part and, using the line you have drawn as a guide, turn the raw edges under all around; baste them flat, as shown in Diagram 3.

Set this piece aside and repeat the basting step with all the other pieces.

11. Center the house on the background piece and pin in place. Pin the other pieces of the picture in place. Baste all the pieces in place and remove the pins. Now appliqué the pieces to the background fabric (see p. 11). Remove the basting.

12. Letting your imagination take over, use the project photograph as a guide and add the details. We used lace for the fences and window shades. We embroidered (see p. 13) leaves, berries, plants, and flowers. You may want to add a sun, rainbow, moon, or other elements to your portrait. If you have never embroidered before, do some practice stitches on scrap fabric first.

13. Have your portrait framed professionally, buy a frame for it, or renew an old frame.

HOLIDAY IDEAS

LOLLIPOP CHRISTMAS TREE ORNAMENTS

Add a new flavor to your Christmas tree with these colorful calico lollipops. These ornaments can be made from scraps of fabric that are only 4 inches square. You can buy a wooden dowel at your lumberyard or craft store to make the sticks or you can save ice cream or popsicle sticks and use them. Each lollipop can be made unique by adding bits of lace, sequins, or embroidery. Try using different fabrics for each side of the lollipop. The directions are to make four lollipops, but you can make as many as you have scraps of fabric.

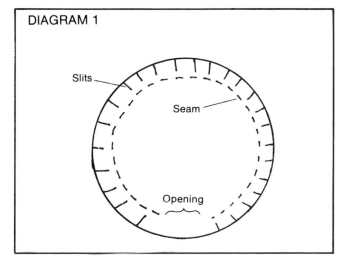

MATERIALS

compass
piece of heavy cardboard, 4 by 4 inches
scissors
8 fabric scraps, each 4 by 4 inches
pencil or fabric marker
straight pins
needle
thread in colors to match fabrics
white glue
small amount of polyester stuffing
1½ feet of wooden dowel, 3/16 inch in diameter, cut into
    four equal lengths
2 feet of ribbon, ¼ inch wide, cut into 6-inch lengths, in
    color to coordinate with fabrics
yarn needle
32 inches of yarn, cut into 8-inch lengths, for hangers

PROCEDURE

1. Using a compass, draw a circle on the cardboard that is 3¼ inches in diameter. Cut the circle out. This is your pattern for cutting the lollipops.

2. Place the cardboard pattern on the wrong side of one of the fabric scraps and trace around it with the pencil or fabric marker. Place the cardboard pattern on another piece of fabric and trace around it. Cut out the fabric rounds on the lines.

3. With right sides of the fabric facing, pin the two fabric pieces together. Allowing a ¼-inch seam allowance, baste the pieces together; remove the pins. Then stitch them together along the seamline, leaving an opening about 1½ inches wide (Diagram 1). Remove the basting.

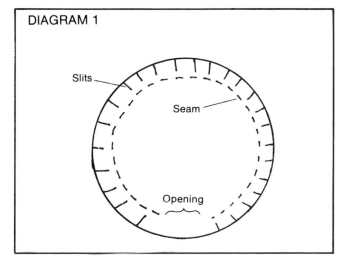

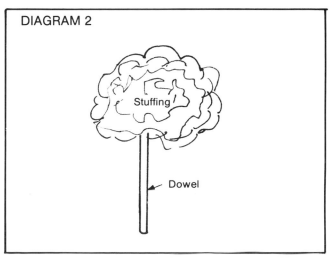

4. Cut slits in the seam allowance all around the fabric edges, as shown in Diagram 1. Turn the piece right side out through the opening.

5. Using the glue, glue a clump of stuffing to the end of one of the pieces of the wooden dowel and set it aside (Diagram 2).

6. Stuff the fabric lollipop with the stuffing. When the lollipop is almost full, push about 1 inch of the end of the dowel with the stuffing glued to it into the opening, as shown in Diagram 3.

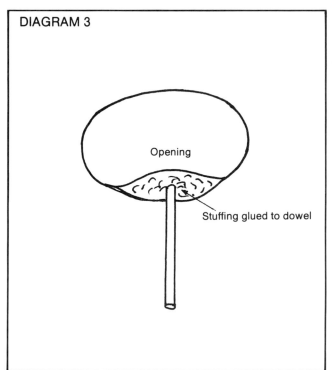

DIAGRAM 3

Opening

Stuffing glued to dowel

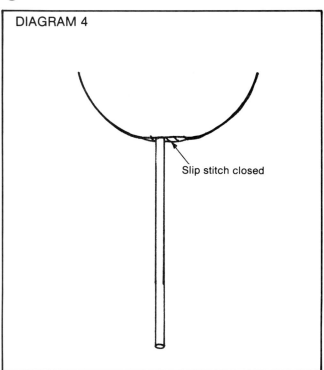

DIAGRAM 4

Slip stitch closed

7. Slip stitch the opening closed around the dowel (Diagram 4). Now the lollipop has a stick.

8. Tie a piece of the ribbon in a bow around the stick, just under the lollipop. Put a dot of glue under the ribbon to prevent it from sliding down the stick.

9. Thread the needle with one of the pieces of yarn. Push the needle through the lollipop near the top and pull the yarn about halfway through. Remove the needle from the yarn and tie the ends in a knot to form a loop to hang the lollipop. Repeat steps 1 through 9 to make three more lollipops with the remaining materials.

2

CHRISTMAS CARD WREATH

Here is the perfect way to make use of those special Christmas cards that you can't bring yourself to throw away. This wreath makes a nice hostess gift for a holiday call or for the children to make for their teachers. It's a great family project because everyone can help with the cutouts and gluing.

MATERIALS

ruler
pencil
compass (optional)
piece of heavy cardboard, 14 by 14 inches
scissors
assorted Christmas cards
white glue
1 yard red ribbon, 3 inches wide, or ¼ yard fabric and
    1 yard fabric fuser (such as Jiffy Fuse or Stitch
    Witchery) for bow

PROCEDURE

1. Using the ruler, pencil, and compass, draw a wreath shape on the cardboard, making the outside circle 14 inches in diameter and the inside circle 8 inches in diameter, as shown in Diagram 1. (If you do not have a compass, you can trace around two circular objects with the correct measurements or you can make your own compass with a piece of string tied around a pencil.)

2. Following the lines you have drawn, cut out the cardboard wreath with the scissors.

3. Cut off the backs of all the Christmas cards and discard them. Cut around the large shapes on the front of the cards, keeping them simple so that the wreath won't look too "busy."

4. Arrange the shapes on the cardboard wreath in a pleasing pattern, overlapping the edges of the cards so that the cardboard background does not show.

5. When you are satisfied with your design, glue the cards in place, using the white glue.

6. If you are using the ribbon, tie it into a bow and glue the bow to the wreath, as shown in the project photograph. If you are using the fabric and fabric joiner to make the bow, cut two strips of fabric, each 4 by 36 inches. Following the directions given by the fabric-fuser manufacturer, join the strips together. Then trim the strip neatly to measure 2½ by 35 inches. Tie a bow of the fabric strip and glue it to the wreath, as shown in the project photograph.

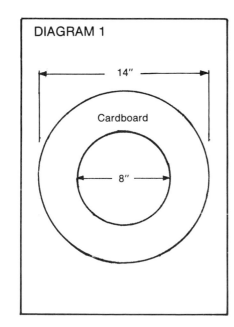

DIAGRAM 1

14″

Cardboard

8″

3

PATCHWORK CHRISTMAS TREE SKIRT

Bring a bit of "Christmas in the country" to your holiday decor with this charming calico patchwork Christmas tree skirt. We used scraps of fabric that were predominately red and green in honor of the season, but the same feeling could be achieved with other colors.

We used an old sheet for the backing. Without the slit, this skirt, which measures about 45 inches in diameter, can become a tablecloth for a round table. For a decorator look, drape a floor-length cloth over the table first.

MATERIALS

piece of heavy cardboard, 6 by 6 inches

scissors

enough scraps of eight different kinds of cotton fabric to make sixty-four 6-inch squares (you will need pieces about 1 by 2 feet of each different fabric)

needle

thread in colors to match fabrics

straight pins

white chalk

string

square of fabric, 45 by 45 inches, in color to coordinate with fabric scraps, for backing

½ yard fabric, 45 inches wide, in color to coordinate with fabric scraps, for ruffle

1½ yards grosgrain ribbon, 1 inch wide, in color to coordinate with fabric

PROCEDURE

1. Using the cardboard square as a pattern, cut sixty-four squares from the fabrics you have chosen, stacking them in separate piles according to color—you should have eight piles. Number them from 1 to 8. Following Diagram 1, lay the squares out, according to number, on a flat surface.

2. Following Diagram 1, with right sides always together, begin sewing the squares in Row 1 together, leaving a ¼-inch seam allowance. Sew the squares in Row 2 together and join Rows 1 and 2. Next sew the squares in Row 3 together and join to Row 2. Continue this process until you have joined all eight rows. Press all seams with an iron.

3. With right sides together, fold the patchwork square in half and lay it on a flat surface. Find the center of the folded edge and mark it with a pin. Tie the chalk to one end of the string and place the chalk at one end of the folded edge. Pull the string taut to the pin in the center. Holding the string on the pin, move the chalk in an arc along the fabric, as shown in Diagram 2. (The string acts like a compass and enables you to draw a half circle on the fabric.)

Cut through both layers of fabric along the chalk line. Unfold the patchwork round.

DIAGRAM 1

Row 1	1	2	3	4	5	6	7	8
Row 2	2	3	4	5	6	7	8	1
Row 3	3	4	5	6	7	8	1	2
Row 4	4	5	6	7	8	1	2	3
Row 5	5	6	7	8	1	2	3	4
Row 6	6	7	8	1	2	3	4	5
Row 7	7	8	1	2	3	4	5	6
Row 8	8	1	2	3	4	5	6	7

DIAGRAM 2

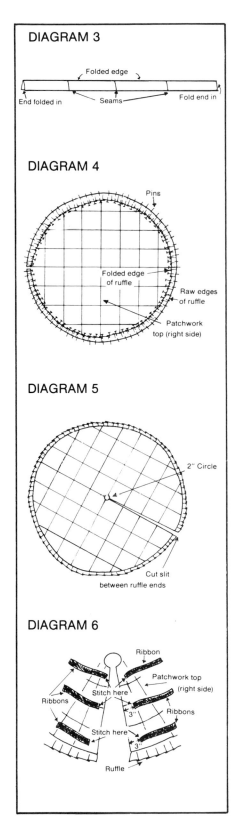

DIAGRAM 3

Folded edge

End folded in   Seams   Fold end in

DIAGRAM 4

Pins

Folded edge
of ruffle

Raw edges
of ruffle

Patchwork
top (right side)

DIAGRAM 5

2" Circle

Cut slit
between ruffle ends

DIAGRAM 6

Ribbon

Patchwork top
(right side)

Stitch here

Ribbons

Ribbons

3"

Stitch here

3"

Ruffle

4. Spread the fabric for the backing on a flat surface. Place the patchwork piece over it. Using it as a pattern, cut the backing fabric for the patchwork around it so that the patchwork piece and backing are the same size.

5. Cut four strips of fabric, each 4 by 45 inches, from the fabric for the ruffle. With right sides together and with a ¼-inch seam allowance, sew the short ends together so that you have one long strip. With wrong sides facing, fold the strip in half lengthwise and press it along the fold. Fold the short ends in ¼ inch and press them flat (Diagram 3).

6. Place the patchwork circle on a flat surface, right side up. Pin the raw edges of the strip for the ruffle in small pleats all around the edge of the patchwork circle on the right side of the fabric, leaving a ½-inch opening where the ends of the ruffle meet (Diagram 4).

7. Stitch the ruffle in place ½ inch in from the edge and remove the pins. Press the ruffle pleats flat.

8. With right sides together, baste the patchwork piece to the backing, following the line of the ruffle stitching. Stitch the pieces together along the basting, leaving a 3-inch opening. Remove the basting and turn the skirt right side out. Slip stitch the opening closed.

9. Press the pleats of the ruffle flat.

10. Find the center of the skirt by folding it in quarters, and mark it. Cut a slit from the ½-inch opening between the ruffle ends to the center of the skirt, as shown in Diagram 5.

Cut a circle 2 inches in diameter in the center (Diagram 5). Turn the raw edges down the slit and around the circle in ¼ inch so that they are between the two layers. Pin, baste, and stitch them to finish the edges. Remove the basting.

11. Cut the grosgrain ribbon in six 9-inch pieces. Following Diagram 6, sew the ribbons on the skirt, equally spaced, 3 inches in from one of the edges of the slit. Sew the remaining three ribbons in place near the other edge of the slit. This will enable the edges of the skirt to overlap when tied.

4

WOODLANDS PINECONE HEART

This heart, fashioned of tiny pine-cones, bright straw flowers, acorns, and small pods glued to a backing, is an easy but elegant project perfect for gift-giving. Warm up a room or the heart of a friend with this creation. The next time you are in pinecone country, take a burlap bag with you and collect woodland resources for making this project.

MATERIALS

brown wrapping paper or other paper for cutting
   pattern
pencil
ruler
scissors
piece of heavy cardboard, 7 by 7 inches
acrylic paint in brown
small paintbrush
paper clip
ice pick
wire cutters
white glue
tiny pinecones (about 1 to 1½ inches long)
small pods
small acorn shells
small straw flowers in the color of your choice
spray varnish

PROCEDURE

1. Using the brown wrapping paper, pencil, and ruler, enlarge the pattern for the cardboard heart (see p. 13). Cut the pattern out of the paper. Place the heart-shaped pattern on top of the cardboard and trace around the pattern.

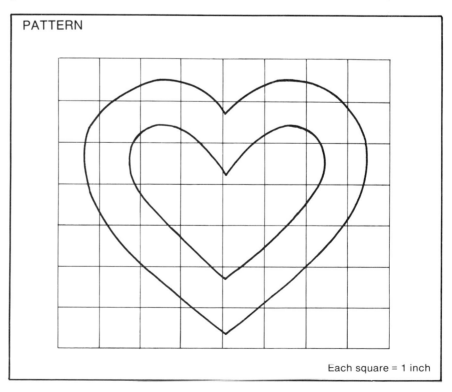

PATTERN

Each square = 1 inch

2. Cut the heart shape out of the cardboard, cutting around the inside heart shape first and then around the outside, as shown in Diagram 1.

3. Paint the cardboard heart with the brown paint and allow it to dry thoroughly.

4. Unbend the paper clip. Using the ice pick, punch two small holes in the top of the heart (Diagram 2). Push one end of the paper clip into one of the holes and bend that end up ¼ inch, as shown in Diagram 2. Push the other end of the clip through the other hole and bend that end up to secure the wire. Snip the excess wire off with the wire cutters. The heart now has a hanger.

5. Using the project photograph as a guide, glue the pinecones, pods, and acorn shells in place, gluing the cones so that they overlap the edges slightly to hide the edge of the cardboard. If you snip some of the pinecones in half across the middle and glue them cut side up, you will get a pretty flower effect (Diagram 3).

6. Snip the stems of the straw flowers near their heads. Glue the flowers in various spots around the heart. Allow all the glue to dry thoroughly.

7. Give the heart several light coats of spray varnish, following the directions on the can. Allow the heart to dry thoroughly.

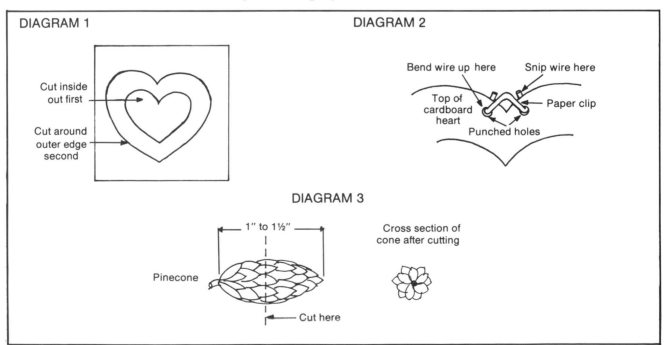

DIAGRAM 1

Cut inside out first

Cut around outer edge second

DIAGRAM 2

Bend wire up here   Snip wire here

Top of cardboard heart

Paper clip

Punched holes

DIAGRAM 3

1" to 1½"

Cross section of cone after cutting

Pinecone

Cut here

5

PINECONE CHRISTMAS WREATH

Collect pinecones for your wreath on a walk through the woods in the fall. Then on a cold evening in December, sit by the fire and put together a beautiful Christmas wreath. We made ours 16 inches in diameter, but if you prefer to make a smaller or larger wreath, simply change the size of the wreath ring you buy and the amount of materials used.

MATERIALS

40 to 45 pinecones, each about 5 inches long
double-ring metal wreath ring, 16 inches in diameter
    (see Diagram 1), available in any nursery
spool of florist's wire
wire cutters
30 to 35 round pinecones, each about 3 inches in
    diameter and about 2 inches long
bunch of dried baby's breath
scissors
masking tape
10 yards plaid ribbon, ¾ inch wide
10 yards velvet ribbon, ¾ inch wide, in red

PROCEDURE

1. Soak the long pinecones in a pail of warm water until their scales close.

2. Slide the cones, one at a time, between the two hoops of the wreath ring (Diagram 1), filling it completely.

Set the ring aside overnight to dry. (When the cones dry, they will open again, which will secure them in the ring.)

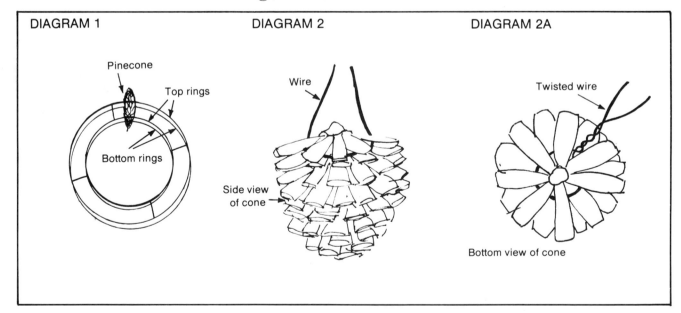

DIAGRAM 1

Pinecone
Top rings
Bottom rings

DIAGRAM 2

Wire
Side view
of cone

DIAGRAM 2A

Twisted wire
Bottom view of cone

3. Wire the round cones to the filled ring by using the following procedure: Cut a piece of florist's wire 8 inches long and bend it in a curve. Slide the bent part of the wire under some of the bottom scales of the pinecone and twist the wire until it is wrapped tightly around the cone, as shown in Diagrams 2 and 2A.

If you want some of your pinecones to look like flowers, just snip the scales off near the top of the cone with the wire cutters and cut off the center core (Diagram 3).

Set all the wired pinecones aside.

4. Separate the baby's breath into eight small bunches, each 5 inches across. Cut the stems of the baby's breath to about 4 inches long. Wrap a piece of masking tape around the stems of each bunch to hold them together (Diagram 4).

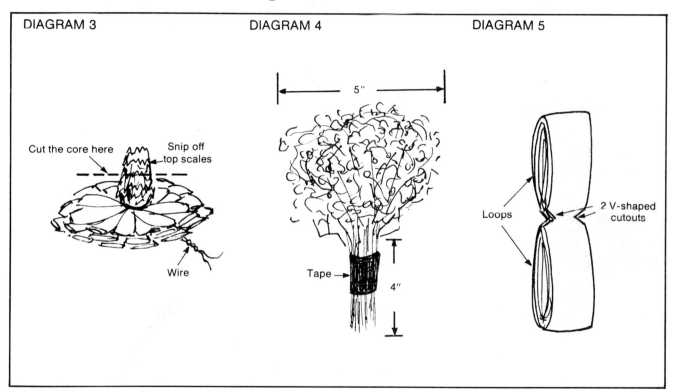

DIAGRAM 3

Cut the core here   Snip off top scales

Wire

DIAGRAM 4

5"

Tape

4"

DIAGRAM 5

Loops

2 V-shaped cutouts

5. Make four bows out of the plaid ribbon and four bows out of the red velvet ribbon, using the following procedure: Loop a piece of ribbon around your hand six times. Snip two V shapes out of the center section of the looped ribbon. The V shapes will be opposite each other, as shown in Diagram 5.

Cut a piece of wire, 8 inches long, and fold it in half. Wrap the folded wire around the section of the looped ribbon where you have cut out the V shapes. Twist the wire behind the ribbon to hold the loops together. Spread the loops of the bow to fluff it, as shown in Diagram 6.

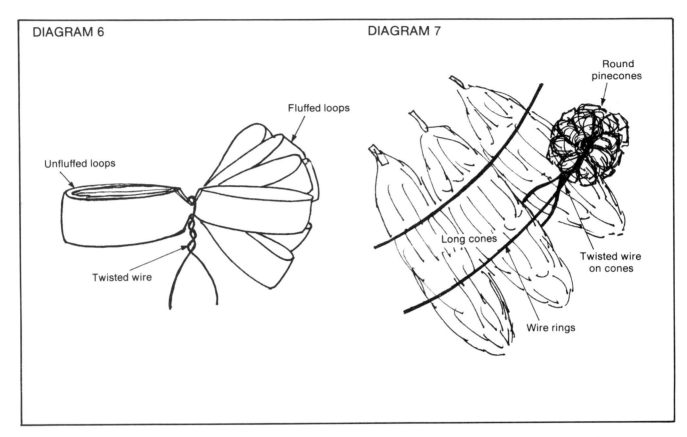

DIAGRAM 6

Fluffed loops

Unfluffed loops

Twisted wire

DIAGRAM 7

Round pinecones

Long cones

Twisted wire on cones

Wire rings

6. Wire the round pinecones to the wreath, as follows: Push the ends of the wire you have twisted around each cone between the metal rings and long cones on the wreath (Diagram 7).

Twist the ends of the wire together on the bottom side of the wreath and snip off the excess with the wire cutters. Bend the ends of the wire back up between two of the long cones so that there will be no sharp ends jutting out.

7. Cut eight pieces of wire, each about 8 inches long. Wrap one 8-inch piece of wire around the stems of each bunch of baby's breath. Following the project photograph for placement, tuck the bunches of baby's breath between the pinecones. Follow the instructions in step 6 to secure the bunches to the wreath.

8. Following the instructions in step 6, wire the bows to the wreath, spacing them evenly around the wreath.

PATCHWORK CHRISTMAS TABLECLOTH

Our gaily patched tablecloth is a versatile size for a variety of tables (about 55 inches square). It will cover a card table, or it can be laid handkerchief-fashion over a round, skirted table, and it even works well placed diagonally on oblong tables of different sizes. Make it in shades of brown and rust for the fall or green and yellow for the springtime.

MATERIALS

piece of heavy cardboard, 3½ by 3½ inches
scissors
about 1/3 yard 45-inch-wide fabric in each of eight
    different red- and green-printed fabrics
needle
thread in color to match border and backing fabric
    (below)
2¾ yards 45-inch-wide fabric for borders and backing, or
    1½ yards of fabric for borders and a bed sheet for backing
pencil
ruler

PROCEDURE

1. Using the cardboard square as a pattern, cut out 32 squares from each of the eight different fabrics, stacking them in separate piles by pattern—you should have eight piles. Number each of the fabrics one through eight. Following Diagram 1 for placement, lay the squares out, according to number, on a flat surface.

DIAGRAM 1

Row 1	1	2	3	4	5	6	7	8	1	2	3	4	5	6	7	8
Row 2	2	3	4	5	6	7	8	1	2	3	4	5	6	7	8	1
Row 3	3	4	5	6	7	8	1	2	3	4	5	6	7	8	1	2
Row 4	4	5	6	7	8	1	2	3	4	5	6	7	8	1	2	3
Row 5	5	6	7	8	1	2	3	4	5	6	7	8	1	2	3	4
Row 6	6	7	8	1	2	3	4	5	6	7	8	1	2	3	4	5
Row 7	7	8	1	2	3	4	5	6	7	8	1	2	3	4	5	6
Row 8	8	1	2	3	4	5	6	7	8	1	2	3	4	5	6	7
Row 9	1	2	3	4	5	6	7	8	1	2	3	4	5	6	7	8
Row 10	2	3	4	5	6	7	8	1	2	3	4	5	6	7	8	1
Row 11	3	4	5	6	7	8	1	2	3	4	5	6	7	8	1	2
Row 12	4	5	6	7	8	1	2	3	4	5	6	7	8	1	2	3
Row 13	5	6	7	8	1	2	3	4	5	6	7	8	1	2	3	4
Row 14	6	7	8	1	2	3	4	5	6	7	8	1	2	3	4	5
Row 15	7	8	1	2	3	4	5	6	7	8	1	2	3	4	5	6
Row 16	8	1	2	3	4	5	6	7	8	1	2	3	4	5	6	7

DIAGRAM 2

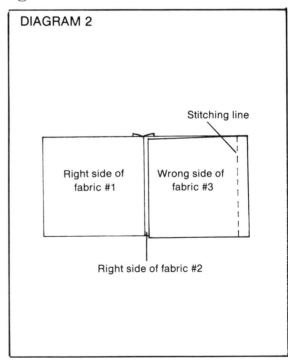

Stitching line

Right side of fabric #1

Wrong side of fabric #3

Right side of fabric #2

2. Following Diagram 1, with right sides always together, begin sewing the squares in Row 1 together, leaving a ¼-inch seam allowance, as shown in Diagram 2. Continue this process until you have joined all sixteen squares in the first row. Press the seams in the row flat.

3. Following Diagram 1, sew the patches of the second row together. Press all the seams flat.

4. With right sides of the fabric facing, pin Row 1 to Row 2, aligning the seams between the patches in each row. Sew the two rows together with a ¼-inch seam (Diagram 3) and remove the pins.

5. Following steps 2 through 4, sew the remaining patches into rows and the rows to each other until you have completed all 16 rows.

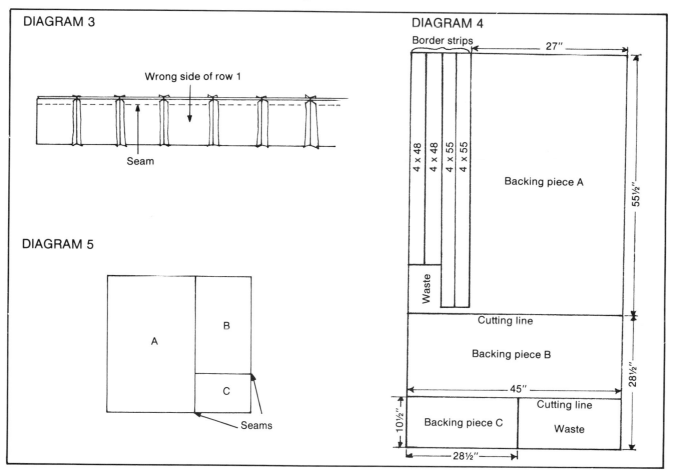

6. If you are using a sheet for the backing, cut from it a 55½-inch square. Then lay out the fabric for the borders and cut two strips, each 4 by 48 inches, and two more strips, each 4 by 55½ inches. If you are using one large piece of fabric for both backing and borders, follow Diagram 4 for cutting out the pieces. Then, with right sides together, sew backing piece C to backing piece B along the two 28½-inch sides with a ¼-inch seam allowance. Then join this piece to backing piece A along the 55½-inch side, again with a ¼-inch seam allowance (Diagram 5). Set this piece aside.

7. Lay the patchwork top of the tablecloth on a flat surface right side up. With right sides together, pin one of the 4- by 48-inch strips of fabric to one of the edges of the patchwork top. Stitch them together with a ¼-inch seam and remove the pins (Diagram 6). Press the seam flat. Repeat this procedure at the opposite edge of the patchwork with the remaining 4- by 48-inch strip of fabric.

8. Pin the two 4- by 55½-inch strips of fabric to the remaining two edges, with right sides together. Stitch them to the patchwork top with a ¼-inch seam and remove the pins (Diagram 7). Press the seams flat.

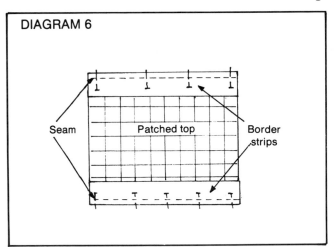

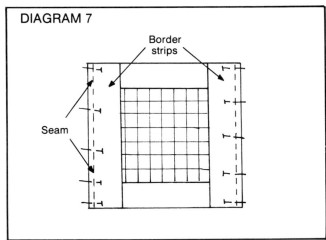

9. Place the patchwork top on a flat surface right side up and place the fabric for the backing right side down on top of it. Pin the edges together and stitch a ¼-inch seam all around the edges of the cloth, leaving a 4-inch opening on one side (Diagram 8). Remove the pins.

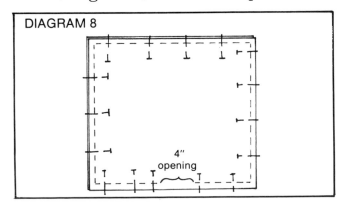

10. Turn the cloth right side out through the opening and slip stitch the opening closed. Press the cloth flat.

4

FOR THE CHILDREN

CHILD'S RAINBOW STOCKING CAP

This colorful, snug cap topped with a perky pom-pom, is a good project for using up leftover yarn. It is cute on its own or great as a set with our leg warmers (see p. 108). We used acrylic yarn, but you can use whatever you have around. Be-cause the pattern is a ribbed one, the cap stretches enough to fit any child's head—just "test knit" with your yarn first to adjust the gauge. Knit away and surprise your favorite little one with this easy-to-make gift!

MATERIALS

leftover 4-ply acrylic yarn in four colors
knitting needles, No. 5
scissors
yarn needle
piece of cardboard, 4 by 4 inches
ruler

Gauge:
6 stitches = 1 inch; 6 rows = 1 inch

Size:
Instructions are given for average-size child's head.

Abbreviations:
k = knit
p = purl
st(s) = stitch(es)

Note: Entire hat is worked in a ribbing stitch (k 2 sts, p 2 sts). Follow Diagram 1 for positioning of colors.

PROCEDURE

1. Cast on 100 stitches.

2. Beginning at the bottom of the hat, work color No. 1 for 22 rows.

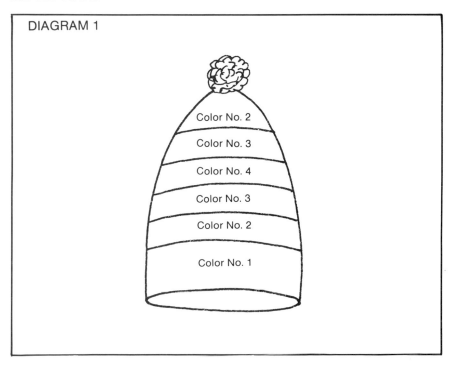

DIAGRAM 1

Color No. 2
Color No. 3
Color No. 4
Color No. 3
Color No. 2
Color No. 1

3. Work color No. 2 for 10 rows.

4. Work color No. 3 for 10 rows.

5. Work color No. 4 for 10 rows.

6. Work color No. 3 for 10 rows.

7. Work color No. 2 for 12 rows, leaving the sts on the needle at the end of the last row.

8. Cut the yarn connecting the hat to the skein approximately 1 yard from the last st (Diagram 2).

9. Thread the yarn needle with the end of the yarn connected to the hat.

10. Begin removing the sts from the knitting needle with the yarn needle onto the yarn (Diagram 3). Start with the st closest to the point of the knitting needle and work across until all 100 sts are on the strand of yarn.

11. The yarn holding the sts at the top of the hat now becomes a drawstring. Push all the sts to the far end of the drawstring as close together as possible to close the top of the hat (Diagram 4). (The small hole remaining at the top where you have gathered the stitches will be covered later with the pom-pom.)

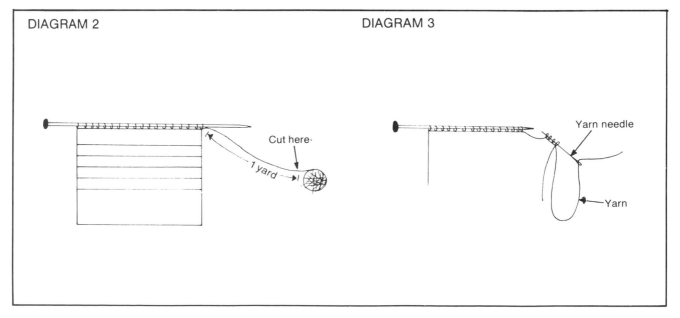

DIAGRAM 2

DIAGRAM 3

12. Turn the hat wrong side out and, starting at the top, overcast the side seam closed, using the remaining drawstring yarn and the yarn needle (Diagram 5). Fasten off and turn the hat right side out.

13. To make the pom-pom: Wind each of the four colors of yarn around the square of cardboard about twenty-five times. Slide the yarn off the cardboard carefully. Cut a piece of yarn (any color) about 10 inches long and tie it around the center of the yarn you have just removed from the cardboard to hold the loops together (Diagram 6).

Cut through all the loops and trim the ends into a round shape. Sew through the tie to fasten the pom-pom to the top of the hat. Turn up a 2-inch cuff around the bottom.

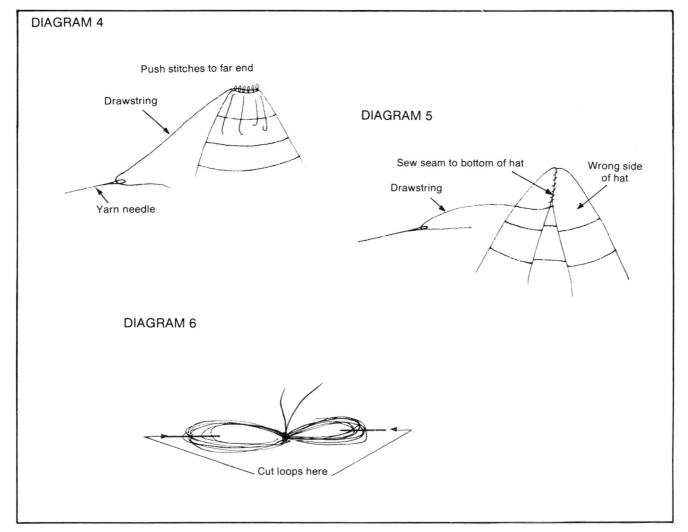

CHILD'S
RAINBOW LEGWARMERS

These bright, toasty legwarmers, which match the rainbow stocking cap on page 104, are a good way to use up many scraps of yarn—one suggestion is to take apart old sweaters, wind the yarn around a solid, flat surface, wet the yarn with cold water, and let it dry. When dry, it will be crinkle-free and ready for knitting. Though designed to fit children from about five to eight years, these legwarmers can be made longer by adding extra rows or shorter by knitting fewer rows.

MATERIALS

leftover 4-ply acrylic yarn in four colors
scissors
knitting needles, No. 3
knitting needles, No. 5
tape measure
straight pins
yarn needle
1 yard flat elastic, ¼ inch wide
safety pin
thread
sewing needle

Gauge:
6 stitches = 1 inch; 6 rows = 1 inch

Size: Instructions are given for children from ages five to eight years old.

Abbreviations:
k = knit
p = purl
st(s) = stitch(es)

Note: The entire project is knitted in a ribbing stitch (k 2 sts, p 2 sts). Follow Diagram 1 for positioning of colors.

PROCEDURE

1. Wind two balls, each the same size, of color No. 1. Repeat this with colors No. 2, No. 3, and No. 4.

2. Cast 66 stitches onto one of the No. 3 knitting needles, using one ball of color No. 1, and cast another 66 stitches onto the same needle, using the second ball of color No. 1. (Both legwarmers will be worked at the same time. Always work 1 row from the first ball and 1 row from the second ball of the same color as you knit.)

3. Beginning at the bottom of the legwarmers: k 2, p 2 for 30 rows.

4. Switch to the No. 5 knitting needles and color No. 2, and k 2, p 2 for 15 rows.

5. Switch to color No. 3, and k 2, p 2 for 15 rows.

6. Switch to color No. 4, and k 2, p 2 for 15 rows.

7. Switch to color No. 3, and k 2, p 2 for 15 rows.

8. Switch to color No. 2, and k 2, p 2 for 25 rows.

9. Switch to color No. 4, and k 2, p 2 for 17 rows.

10. Bind off all the stitches on both legwarmers, leaving about 1 yard of the yarn from each ball still attached to the knitting. This will be used to sew the back seams (Diagram 2).

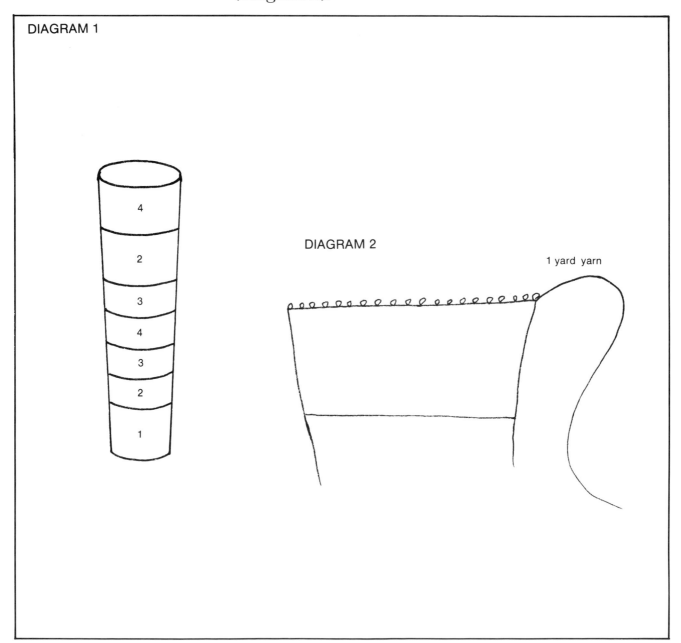

DIAGRAM 1

DIAGRAM 2

1 yard yarn

11. Turn the legwarmers inside out and pin the edges at each color change, using the straight pins (Diagram 3).

12. Using the yarn needle and the piece of yarn you have left attached, sew the seam together on each legwarmer.

13. On one of the legwarmers, turn the top (the last color you knitted) down ¾ inch all around, to the inside of the legwarmer. With the yarn needle and some of the color No. 4 yarn, stitch the edge down all the way around the top of the legwarmer, leaving a ½-inch opening.

14. Cut a piece of elastic 10 inches long and pin the safety pin to one end of it. Push the pin through the gap in the casing you have just made at the top of the legwarmer. Continue pushing it all the way around until it comes back out through the gap. Cut off any excess elastic, overlap the ends, and sew them together with the sewing needle and thread.

15. Sew the hole in the casing closed, using a piece of color No. 4 yarn and the yarn needle.

16. Repeat steps 13 through 15 with the other legwarmer.

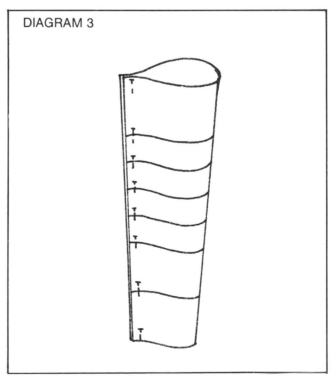

DIAGRAM 3

17. Cut a 6-inch piece of elastic. Place one of the legwarmers on a flat surface and flatten it out so that the seam is in the middle (Diagram 4).

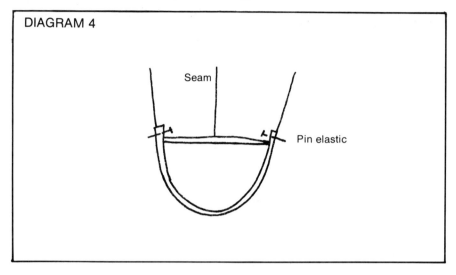

DIAGRAM 4

Seam

Pin elastic

18. Using the straight pins, pin each end of the elastic to the outside edges of the bottom of the legwarmer, as shown in Diagram 4.

19. Sew the ends in place with the sewing needle and thread, concealing the stitches so that the thread will not show on the right side of the legwarmer. Turn the legwarmer right side out.

20. Repeat steps 17 through 19 with the other legwarmer.

3

CHILD'S PAINTING SMOCK

Save an outdated man's shirt and fabric scraps left over from another project to make this smock—a very handy thing to have around for little people to wear while they are doing all sorts of projects, from painting to baking. You might make a number of them to sell at the next PTA fund raiser or for the next bazaar.

MATERIALS

one adult-sized man's shirt
scissors
thread in color to match shirt
needle
about ½ yard 45-inch-wide fabric for trim
straight pins
brown wrapping paper or other paper for cutting
   pattern
ruler
pencil
fabric marker (optional)
2 feet of rickrack, standard size, in color to coordinate
   with shirt
two 7-inch-long pieces of elastic, ¼ inch wide
large safety pin
small safety pin

PROCEDURE

1. Cutting just above the neck band, cut the collar from the shirt, as shown in Diagram 1.

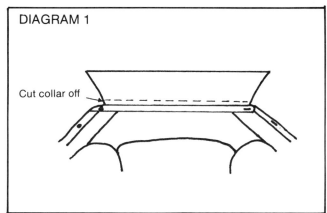

DIAGRAM 1

Cut collar off

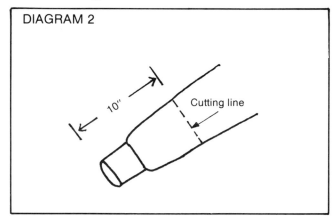

DIAGRAM 2

10"

Cutting line

2. Cut off the shirt sleeves about 10 inches from the end of the cuff, as shown in Diagram 2.

3. Cut off the buttonhole placket and the strip with the buttons sewn to it, as shown in Diagram 3. Sew a ¼-inch hem along the opening on both sides.

4. Cut a piece of trimming fabric 4 by 45 inches (if necessary, join pieces to make this length). With the wrong sides of the fabric facing, fold it in half lengthwise. Stitch a ¼-inch seam at both ends, as shown in Diagram 4. Turn the strip right side out and press along the fold. This strip will become the neck band and neck ties.

5. Lay the shirt out, right side up, on a flat surface. With right sides facing, center and pin one of the raw edges of the neck band you have just sewn along the line of stitching that attaches the neck band to the shirt (Diagram 5). Baste the neck band in place and remove the pins. Following the line of stitching on the old neck band, stitch the new neck band to the old one with a ¼-inch seam. Remove the basting.

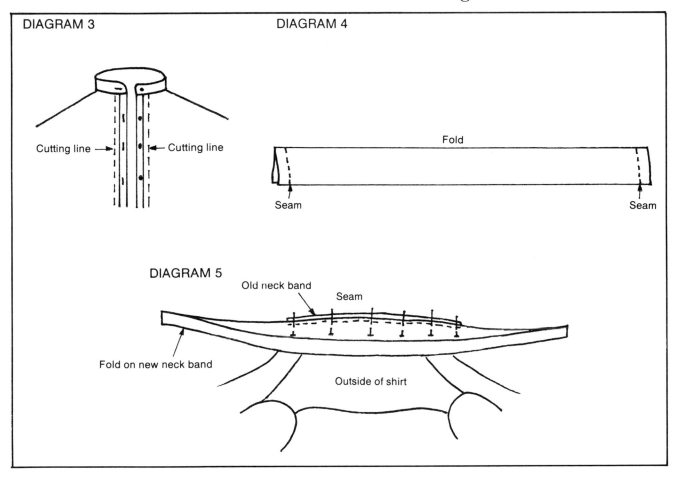

DIAGRAM 3

Cutting line → ← Cutting line

DIAGRAM 4

Fold

Seam   Seam

DIAGRAM 5

Old neck band

Seam

Fold on new neck band

Outside of shirt

6. Fold the new neck band over the old one. Turn the raw edges ¼ inch to the inside along the entire length of the new neck band and pin them. Baste the edges, remove the pins, and then slip stitch the edges closed (Diagram 6). Remove the basting.

7. Cut two more strips of the trimming fabric (for the ties in the middle of the smock), each 4 by 24 inches. Fold them in half lengthwise, right sides facing. Stitch them along one short edge and the long edge with a ¼-inch seam, as shown in Diagram 7.

8. Pin about 1¼ inches of the open end of each tie to the opening of the shirt on the wrong side of the shirt about 10 inches down from the neck-band ties (Diagram 8). Stitch them in place and remove the pins.

9. Using the brown paper, ruler, and pencil, enlarge the pattern (see p. 13) for the heart-shaped pocket. Cut the pattern out of the brown paper and pin it to a piece of the trimming fabric. Trace around it with the fabric marker or pencil. Cut the heart out of the fabric.

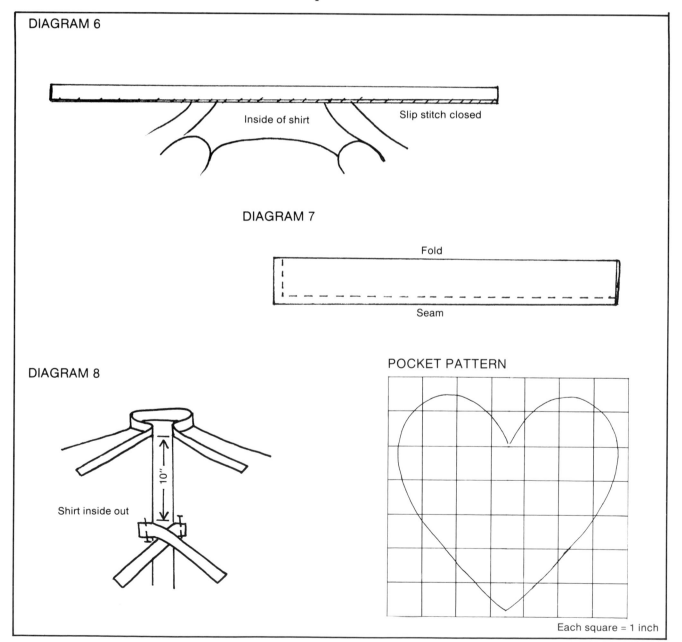

DIAGRAM 6

Inside of shirt   Slip stitch closed

DIAGRAM 7

Fold

Seam

DIAGRAM 8

10"

Shirt inside out

POCKET PATTERN

Each square = 1 inch

10. Turn the raw edges under ¼ inch all around the heart, and baste them in place. Baste the rickrack on the wrong side around the heart shape. Stitch the rickrack to the heart and remove the basting.

11. Using the color photograph as a guide for placement, pin the heart shape to the shirt. Baste the heart in place and remove the pins. Stitch the heart to the shirt, leaving an opening in the top, as shown in Diagram 9. This is now a pocket.

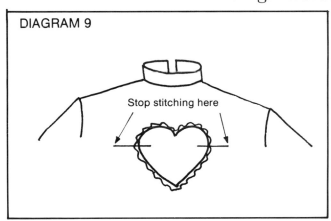

DIAGRAM 9

Stop stitching here

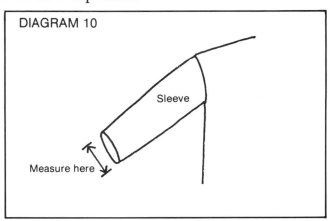

DIAGRAM 10

Sleeve

Measure here

12. Lay one of the sleeves on a flat surface. Measure the width of the sleeve where you have cut off the cuff (Diagram 10). Double this measurement and add ½ inch to it. This number will be the length of the pieces of fabric you will cut for the cuffs. Make the depth 4 inches long. Cut two pieces of trimming fabric to these measurements.

13. Fold one of the pieces of fabric in half widthwise with right sides of the fabric facing. Stitch a ¼-inch seam along the 4-inch ends (Diagram 11). Repeat this procedure with the other piece of fabric. These will become the cuffs.

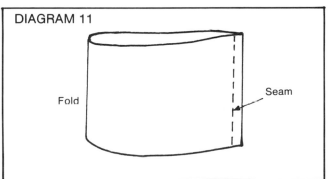

DIAGRAM 11

Fold

Seam

14. With right sides facing, slide one of the cuffs over the end of one of the sleeves. Pin the cuff in place, lining the seam of the cuff up with the seam of the sleeve (Diagram 12). Stitch the cuff to the end of the sleeve with a ¼-inch seam. Remove the pins and fold the cuff down.

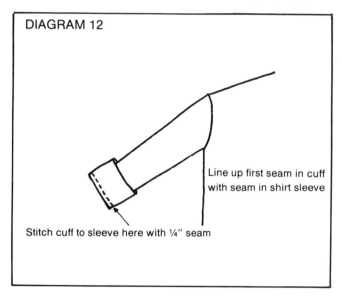

DIAGRAM 12

Line up first seam in cuff with seam in shirt sleeve

Stitch cuff to sleeve here with ¼″ seam

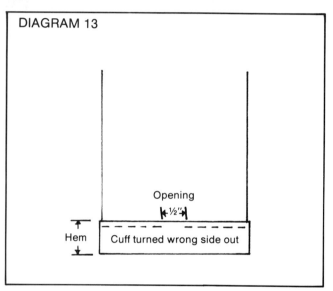

DIAGRAM 13

Opening

|←½″→|

Hem

Cuff turned wrong side out

15. Sew a ½-inch hem along the bottom edge of the cuff, leaving a ½-inch opening in the hem, as shown in Diagram 13.

16. Pin the large safety pin to one of the pieces of elastic. Pin the small safety pin to the other end of the elastic. Push the small safety pin into the opening you have left in the hem of the cuff. Slide it through the hem and push it back out of the opening. Stitch the two ends of the elastic together and remove the safety pins. Slip stitch the opening in the hem to close it.

17. Repeat steps 14, 15, and 16 with the other piece of cuff fabric and elastic.

4

BASKET DOLL CRADLE

Tuck a favorite doll into this cradle, which can be made from a produce basket from the market or even an old Easter basket. Although we use a prequilted fabric for all the pieces except the skirt, you may want, for nostalgic reasons, to use a dress your little girl has outgrown. The eyelet might come from one of her pinafores. If you don't have enough of one kind of fabric to cover the whole basket, you might use a contrasting fabric to line the inside.

MATERIALS

rectangular-shaped basket with a handle
fabric for lining, skirt, mattress, pillow, and blanket (see Note)
tape measure
pencil or fabric marker
scissors
straight pins
thread in colors to match fabrics
needle
white glue
19 inches pregathered eyelet lace in white
flat elastic, ¼ inch wide (see Note)
one large safety pin
one small safety pin
small amount of polyester stuffing (see Note)

Note: The exact amount of fabric, elastic, and stuffing has not been given, for it will vary according to the size of your basket.

PROCEDURE

To cover the basket:
1. Start by lining the basket. Measure the outside surfaces of the basket (two sides, two ends, and the bottom), as shown in Diagram 1. According to your measurements, cut two rectangles of fabric for each side surface, two for each end, and one for the bottom (Diagram 1).

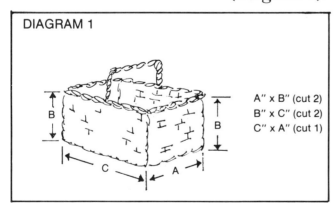

A" x B" (cut 2)
B" x C" (cut 2)
C" x A" (cut 1)

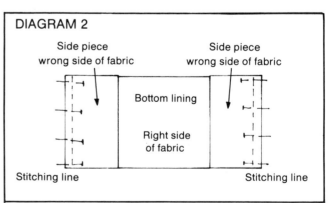

2. Right side up, place the fabric rectangle for lining the bottom of the basket on a flat surface. Place one rectangle for the end on top, right side down, and pin it along the edge. Baste along the edge with a ¼-inch seam allowance, remove the pins, and stitch along the basting line (Diagram 2). Remove the basting. Repeat this procedure on the opposite side.

120

3. Fold the two ends outward. Now place the lining rectangle for one of the long sides on top, right side down, and pin along the edge. Baste it in place, remove the pins, and stitch it in place; remove the basting. Fold this piece out and repeat with the remaining rectangle (Diagram 3).

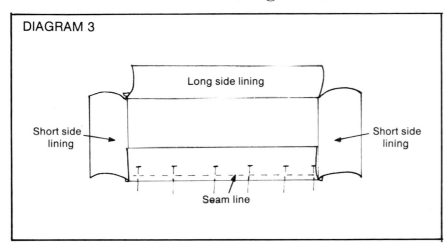

DIAGRAM 3

Long side lining

Short side lining

Short side lining

Seam line

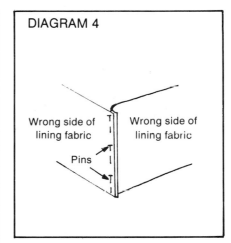

DIAGRAM 4

Wrong side of lining fabric

Wrong side of lining fabric

Pins

4. Bring two adjoining side pieces of the fabric up to meet at one corner and, right side to right side, pin them to each other, as shown in Diagram 4. Baste along the edge and then stitch the seam with a ¼-inch seam. Remove the basting.

Repeat this procedure at the other three corners to form the lining.

5. Place the lining inside the basket. It should be slightly higher than the basket. Cut a wedge of fabric about 1 inch deep out of the lining on each side of the point where the handle is attached to the basket, as shown in Diagram 5.

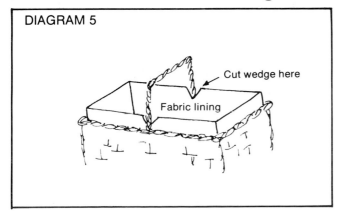

DIAGRAM 5

Cut wedge here

Fabric lining

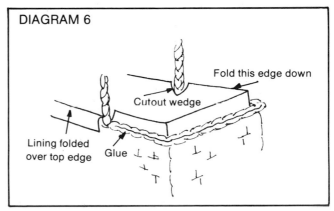

DIAGRAM 6

Fold this edge down

Cutout wedge

Lining folded over top edge

Glue

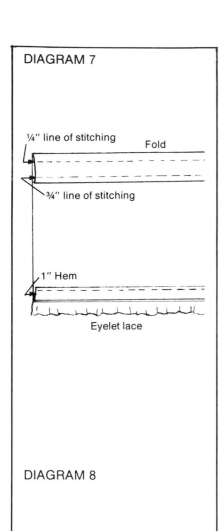

DIAGRAM 7

¼" line of stitching   Fold

¾" line of stitching

1" Hem

Eyelet lace

DIAGRAM 8

Wrong side
of skirt fabric

Seam

6. Spread a line of white glue along the top edge of the basket. Fold the lining over the top edge and press it down over the glue (Diagram 6).

7. Next make the skirt for the basket. Measure around the outside of the basket with the tape measure and double the number. Measure the depth of the basket and add 2 inches to this number. This will give you the dimensions for the skirt fabric. Example: Our basket measures 42 inches around and 5 inches deep, so we needed a piece of fabric 84 by 7 inches. (Since we were using scrap fabric, we had to cut two pieces and join them with a seam at the short ends.) Cut a piece of fabric or join enough pieces to make the size of your measurements.

8. Place the piece of fabric wrong side up on a flat surface. Fold the fabric down 1 inch along the top edge and press the fold flat. Sew a line of stitching ¼ inch down from the folded edge and another line ¾ inch down to form a casing for the elastic, as shown in Diagram 7. Turn in a 1-inch hem along the bottom edge and stitch it down. Sew the straight edge of the eyelet to the right side of the fabric along the stitching line for the hem, as shown in Diagram 7.

9. Fold the fabric in half widthwise, with the right sides of the fabric facing, so that the two short ends meet. Stitch a ½-inch seam along the short ends from the bottom to just below the casing, as shown in Diagram 8.

10. Measure around the outside top edge of the basket. Cut a piece of elastic to the length of this measurement. Pin the large safety pin to one end of the elastic and the small safety pin to the other end. Push the small pin into the casing and work it through to the other end to gather the fabric (the large pin will prevent the other end from slipping through). Remove the small pin and use it to pin the two ends of the elastic together. Remove the large safety pin and sew the two ends of the elastic together. Remove the small pin (Diagram 9).

11. Turn the skirt right side out. Place the skirt around the basket and arrange the gathers evenly. Stitch the skirt to the top of the lining in a few spots along the gathers to prevent the skirt from slipping off.

To make the mattress:

12. Measure the bottom of the basket lengthwise and widthwise. Cut two rectangles of fabric to this size. Place them on top of each other with right sides facing. Stitch a ½-inch seam all the way around the edge of the rectangles, leaving a 3-inch opening on one side. Turn the mattress right side out through the opening and stuff it with the polyester stuffing. Slip stitch the opening closed. Place the mattress in the bottom of the basket.

To make the pillow:

13. Cut two 4- by 5-inch rectangles of fabric. Place one of the rectangles on a flat surface, right side up. Cut a piece of eyelet lace 19 inches long. Pin the straight edge of the lace around the edge of the rectangle, pinning it to the right side of the fabric, as shown in Diagram 10.

14. Lay the second rectangle of fabric on top of the first with the right sides of the fabric facing. Baste the rectangles together with a ½-inch seam allowance and remove the pins. Stitch the rectangles together with the eyelet between them, leaving a 3-inch opening on one side; remove the basting. Turn the pillow right side out through the opening. Stuff the pillow with the polyester stuffing and slip stitch the opening closed.

To make the coverlet:

15. Cut two rectangles of fabric the same size as you used for the mattress. Repeat the steps you used to make the pillow, but omit the stuffing.

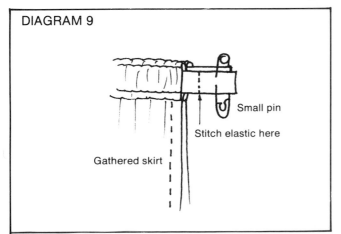

DIAGRAM 9

Small pin

Stitch elastic here

Gathered skirt

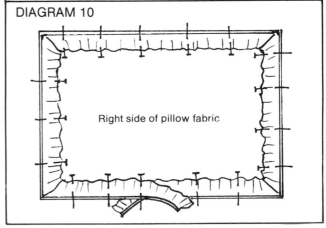

DIAGRAM 10

Right side of pillow fabric

5

LITTLE HELPER'S
TOOL APRON

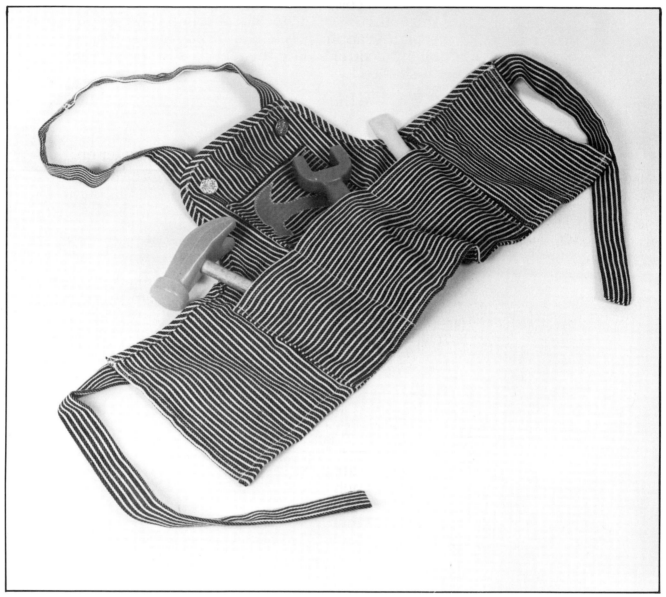

Outfitted in his or her miniature carpenter's apron, complete with a set of bright plastic tools from the local five-and-ten-cent store, your child will love working alongside Dad on his latest home-repair project. Made out of a pair of outgrown toddler's overalls, this apron was fashioned from a blue- and white-striped fabric, but any color of overalls will do. If it's the time of year to start the vegetable garden, you might fill the pockets of the apron with garden tools and a package of seeds.

MATERIALS

one pair of toddler-size overalls
scissors
ruler
straight pins
needle
thread in color to match overalls
pencil
brown wrapping paper or other paper for cutting pattern
piece of cotton fabric, 4 by 5 inches, in red

PROCEDURE

1. Remove the hooks from the straps of the overalls.

2. Cut the legs and back bib off the overalls, as shown in Diagram 1. Set the legs aside to be used later on.

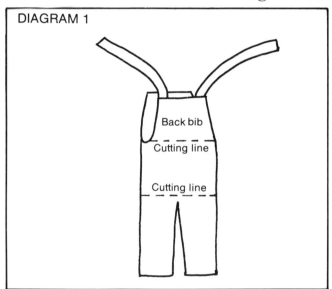

DIAGRAM 1

Back bib

Cutting line

Cutting line

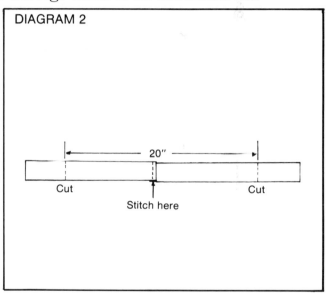

DIAGRAM 2

20"

Cut

Stitch here

Cut

3. Cut the straps off the overalls. Overlap the ends of the straps ½ inch and sew them together with slip stitches, as shown in Diagram 2. Trim the ends so that the strap will be 20 inches long, keeping the ends of the straps you have sewn together in the center of the 20-inch length.

4. Pin the ends of the strap to the top inside edge of the front bib so that the ends of the strap extend 1 inch behind the bib. Sew the ends of the strap in place, as shown in Diagram 3. Leave the buttons in place.

5. Cut the back seam of the overalls open, turn the raw edges under ¼ inch, and sew them in place, as shown in Diagram 4.

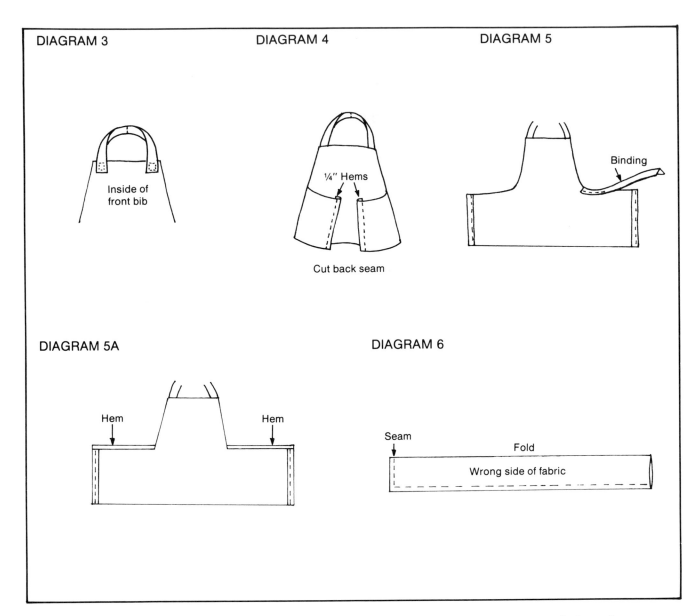

DIAGRAM 3

DIAGRAM 4

DIAGRAM 5

Inside of
front bib

¼" Hems

Cut back seam

Binding

DIAGRAM 5A

DIAGRAM 6

Hem

Hem

Seam

Fold

Wrong side of fabric

6. If the overalls have self-binding around the edges, carefully remove the binding from the back bib you cut off earlier and use it to rebind the top raw edge on the back of the apron (see Diagram 5).

If the overalls do not have binding, turn the raw edge down ¼ inch to the wrong side and hem it (Diagram 5A).

7. Cut two strips of fabric, each 2½ by 15 inches, from one of the overall legs you cut off earlier. With right sides of the fabric facing, fold one of the strips in half lengthwise and stitch a ¼-inch seam along the long edge and one of the short edges, as shown in Diagram 6.

126

DIAGRAM 7

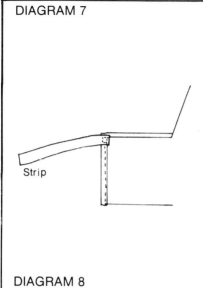

Strip

DIAGRAM 8

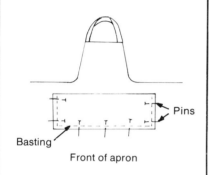

Pins

Basting

Front of apron

HAMMER PATTERN

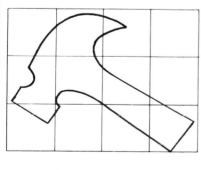

Each square = 1 inch

8. Turn the strip right side out through the open end and pin the raw end of it to one of the edges of the back of the apron so that the raw edge extends ½ inch behind the edge of the fabric (Diagram 7). Stitch the strip in place and remove the pins. Repeat steps 7 and 8 with the second strip of fabric.

9. Hem the bottom edge of the apron with a ½-inch hem.

10. Cut a piece of fabric 6 by 12 inches for the large front pocket. Sew a ¼-inch hem along one 12-inch side; this will be the top of the pocket. Turn the raw edges under ¼ inch on the remaining three sides and baste them in place. Center the tool pocket on the front of the apron and pin it in place. Baste around the side and bottom edges ¼ inch in from the edge, as shown in Diagram 8. Remove the pins and stitch the side and bottom edges, following the basting line. Remove the basting.

11. Following the project photograph for placement, stitch two equally spaced lines of stitching to divide the pocket into three sections.

12. Using the brown wrapping paper, ruler, and pencil, enlarge the pattern (see p. 13) for the hammer appliqué. Cut the pattern out of the paper.

13. Place the red cotton fabric right side up. Place the hammer pattern on top of it and trace around it neatly. Adding ¼ inch all around for a seam allowance, cut around the shape.

14. Cut a piece of the overall fabric 3½ by 5 inches for the top pocket. Appliqué (see p. 11) the hammer shape to the center of it, following the project photograph for placement. Hem one of the 5-inch sides of the pocket with a ¼-inch hem. Center the pocket on the front of the bib with the hemmed side at the top and pin the other three sides in place to the bib, turning the raw edges under ¼ inch as you pin them. Baste along the side and bottom edges ¼ inch in from the edges and remove the pins. Stitch the three edges in place, following the basting lines, and remove the basting. Fill the pockets with plastic tools.

6

CHILD'S SAIL-AWAY WALL HANGING

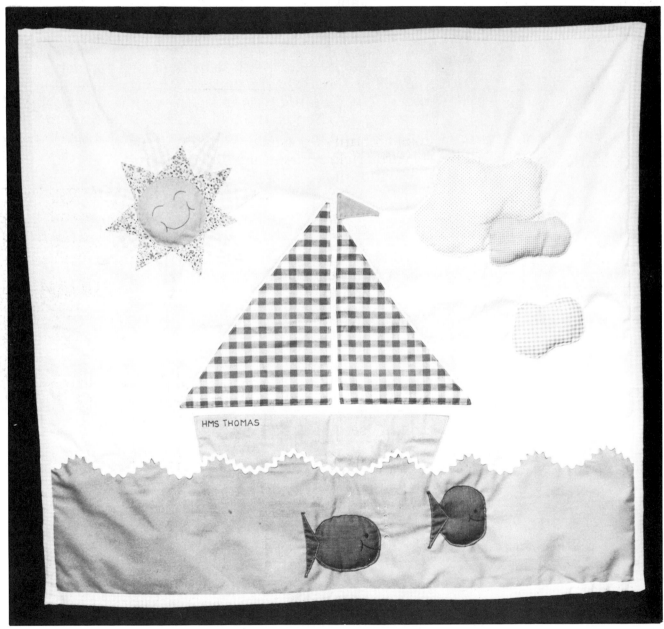

Have fun coordinating fabric scraps you have on hand to create your own color scheme for this whimsical wall hanging featuring a gingham sailboat lazily adrift on a sea of smiling sunfish, or follow the directions given for our wall hanging. Christen the boat with the name of your favorite little sailor.

MATERIALS

brown wrapping paper or other paper for cutting
    patterns
pencil
ruler
scissors
scraps of fabric for appliqués
straight pins
fabric marker (optional)
piece of fabric, 11½ by 42½ inches, in blue, for water
piece of fabric, 39 by 42½ inches, for background
needle
thread in colors to match fabrics
pointed nail scissors
small amount of polyester stuffing
1¾ yards rickrack, standard size, in white
small amounts of embroidery floss in dark blue, yellow,
    and rust
embroidery needle
piece of batting, 39 by 42½ inches
old bedsheet or piece of fabric, 39 by 42½ inches, for
    backing
quilting thread in white
quilting needle
1½ yards fabric for border, in contrasting color
42-inch strip of Velcro, ½ inch wide
small nails

PROCEDURE

1. Using the brown wrapping paper, pencil, and ruler,
enlarge the patterns for the appliqués on the wall
hanging (see p. 13) and cut them out.

2. Select the fabrics you plan to use for each appliqué. (If
the fabrics are wrinkled, press them flat.) Place one
pattern piece on the right side of one of the fabric pieces.
Pin the pattern in place on the right side of one of the
fabric pieces and trace around it with a pencil or the
fabric marker. Add ¼ inch all around and cut out the
pieces (Diagram 1).

Remove the paper pattern from the fabric. Repeat steps
1 and 2 with the rest of the pattern pieces and set
them aside.

3. Cut an 11½- by 42½-inch piece of blue fabric for the
"water." Following the project photograph and the paper
pattern as guides, use the fabric marker or a pencil to
draw the "waves" near the top of the "water." Cut the

PATTERN

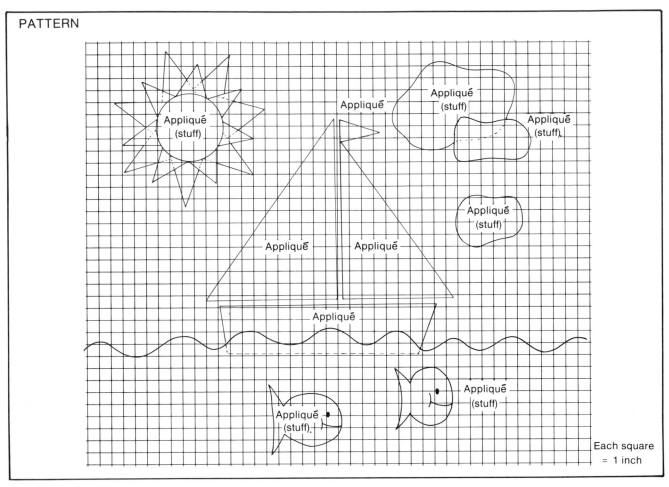

Appliqué
(stuff)

Appliqué
(stuff)

Appliqué

Appliqué
(stuff)

Appliqué
(stuff)

Appliqué

Appliqué

Appliqué

Appliqué
(stuff)

Appliqué
(stuff)

Each square
= 1 inch

DIAGRAM 1

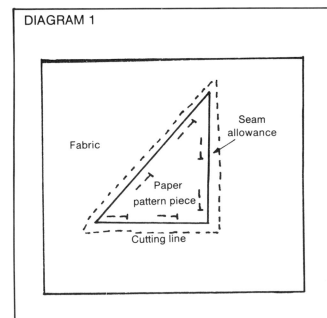

Fabric

Seam
allowance

Paper
pattern piece

Cutting line

DIAGRAM 2

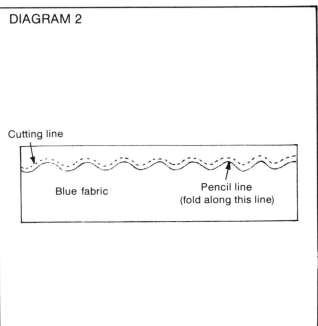

Cutting line

Blue fabric

Pencil line
(fold along this line)

130

DIAGRAM 3

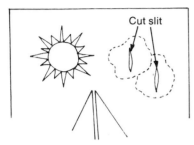

Cut slit

Back side of wall hanging

DIAGRAM 4

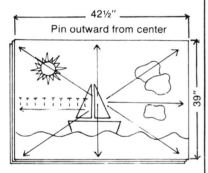

42½"
Pin outward from center

39"

DIAGRAM 5

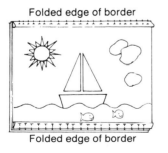

Folded edge of border

Folded edge of border

fabric about ½ inch above the line you just drew, as shown in Diagram 2.

Following the line you have drawn, turn the edges along the "waves" under to the wrong side of the fabric and, clipping the curves so that the edges lie flat, baste them in place. Repeat, turning under and basting the edges of all the appliqué pieces you have cut out.

4. If the background fabric is wrinkled, press it flat. Following the project photograph and pattern, pin all the pieces for the boat, fish, the top and lower clouds, and the outer points of the sun in place on the right side of the fabric, baste, remove the pins, and then appliqué. Because these pieces are so large, we used the sewing machine to appliqué, but it can be done by hand (see p. 11). Remove the basting. Then add the middle cloud and the inner points of the sun. Finally, add the center of the sun.

5. Turn the wall hanging back side up. Locate the wrong side of each of the pieces marked on the pattern to be stuffed. Using nail scissors, cut a slit in the background fabric of each, being careful not to cut through the appliqué, as shown in Diagram 3. Stuff each form with enough of the polyester filling that it is puffy and then loosely stitch the slits closed.

Repeat this step with the rest of the appliqués that are to be stuffed (when you stuff the fish, you will have to cut through two layers of fabric).

6. Turn the wall hanging front side up. Pin the rickrack to the top of the "waves." Baste and stitch it in place. Remove the basting.

7. Carefully write the child's name on the boat with the fabric marker or pencil. Embroider over it in the outline stitch in dark blue (see p. 12). Using the project photograph as a guide, embroider the fish bubbles in yellow and the face on the sun in rust, all in the outline stitch.

8. Place the piece of batting on top of the sheet or other fabric, wrong side up, for the backing. Place the wall hanging front side up on top of the batting. Pin the three layers together, beginning from the center out to one edge and placing the pins about 6 inches apart, as shown in Diagram 4.

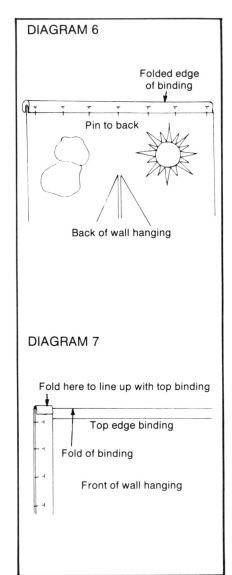

DIAGRAM 6

Folded edge
of binding

Pin to back

Back of wall hanging

DIAGRAM 7

Fold here to line up with top binding

Top edge binding

Fold of binding

Front of wall hanging

Now pin from the center to the opposite edge and, following the arrows in Diagram 4, pin rows in all eight directions. Baste the three layers together along the rows of pins. Remove the pins.

9. Quilt (see p. 14) the three layers of fabric around the appliquéd shapes. Remove the basting.

10. Cut four strips of fabric, two 3 by 39 inches, and two 3 by 42½ inches, from the border fabric. With wrong sides facing, fold the strips in half lengthwise and press each one flat. Pin the raw edges of one of the 42½-inch-long strips to the top and one to the bottom edge on the front of the wall hanging, as shown in Diagram 5. Baste and stitch the binding in place with a ½-inch seam. Remove the basting.

11. Turn the wall hanging over so that it is back side up. Fold the binding at the top over the raw edges of the three layers. Pin the binding in place on the back of the wall hanging, as shown in Diagram 6.

Baste the binding to the back of the wall hanging and remove the pins. Slip stitch and remove the basting. Repeat this step with the bottom binding. Trim the binding at the ends so that it is the same length as the wall hanging.

12. Turn the wall hanging over so that the front side is up and pin the raw edges of one of the 39-inch-long binding strips to the front side along one of the side edges. Baste the strip in place with a ½-inch seam allowance and remove the pins. Stitch along the basting line; remove the basting. Fold the binding in at the ends to line up with the top and bottom edges, as shown in Diagram 7. Fold the side binding over the raw edges of the three layers and baste in place on the back of the hanging. Repeat step 12 on the other side edge. Slip stitch the ends of the binding closed to finish the wall hanging.

13. Pull the Velcro strip apart and sew one half to the back of the wall hanging along the top edge, sewing only through the back layer of fabric so that the stitches will not show on the front. Nail the other half of the Velcro strip to the wall. Press the strips together to hang the wall hanging.

7

RED PLAID
BABY BUNTING

This warm bunting is made from a discarded wool pleated skirt. The plaid is a nice change from the usual pastel-colored baby outfits, and the calico lining makes it soft next to baby's skin.

Another source of fabric for this project could be a soft, plaid flannel bathrobe. Made with loving care, this project makes a wonderful baby-shower gift.

MATERIALS

seam ripper or single-edged razor blade
scissors
one adult-sized pleated skirt, in red plaid
brown wrapping paper or other paper for cutting
  pattern
pencil
ruler
straight pins
1½ yards calico fabric for lining, in blue
thread in color to match plaid fabric
needle
small safety pin
1 yard grosgrain ribbon, ¼ inch wide, in navy blue
5 large snaps

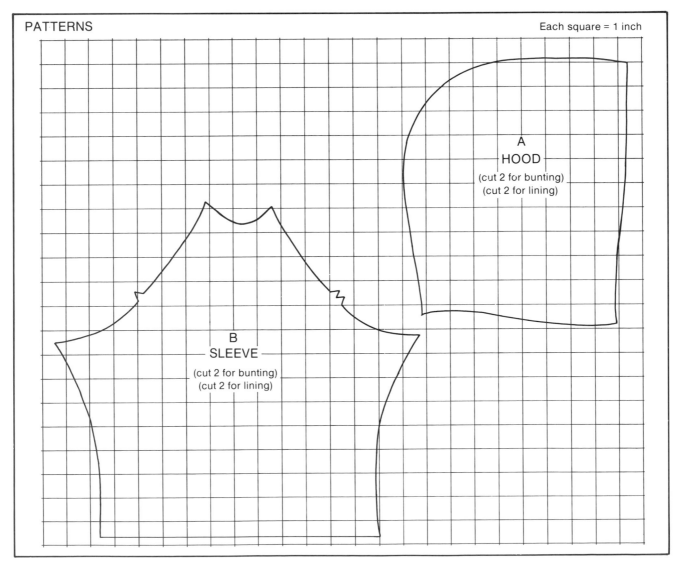

PATTERNS   Each square = 1 inch

A
HOOD
(cut 2 for bunting)
(cut 2 for lining)

B
SLEEVE
(cut 2 for bunting)
(cut 2 for lining)

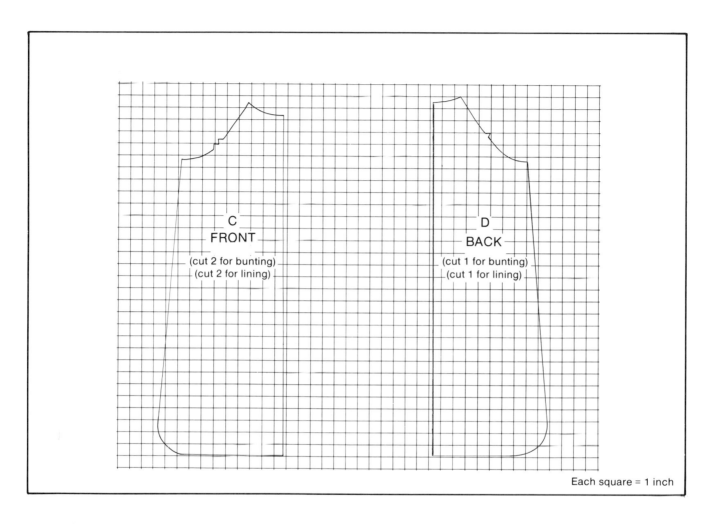

C
FRONT

(cut 2 for bunting)
(cut 2 for lining)

D
BACK

(cut 1 for bunting)
(cut 1 for lining)

Each square = 1 inch

PROCEDURE

1. Using the seam ripper or razor blade and the scissors, remove the waistband from the skirt, take out the pleats, and let down the hem. Lay the piece of fabric, right side facing up, out on a flat surface (press with an iron if necessary).

2. Using the brown wrapping paper, ruler, and pencil, enlarge the pattern pieces (see p. 13). Cut the pattern pieces out of the paper.

3. Fold the plaid fabric in half so that the right sides are together (Diagram 1) and place the pattern pieces on it, following the layout in Diagram 1. Pin the pieces in place and cut around them with the scissors. (Note the instructions on the pattern pieces for the number of each to cut.)

4. Repeat step 3 with the calico lining fabric.

5. Set the plaid pieces aside and work with the calico lining pieces first. Starting with the pieces marked B, C, and D, remove the paper patterns from the fabric. With right sides of the fabric facing, pin one sleeve (B) to the back (D) and one front piece (C), being sure to match the notches. Baste the sleeve in place, remove the pins, and stitch a ½-inch seam. Remove the basting (Diagram 2).

Repeat this step to join the other sleeve and front piece to the back.

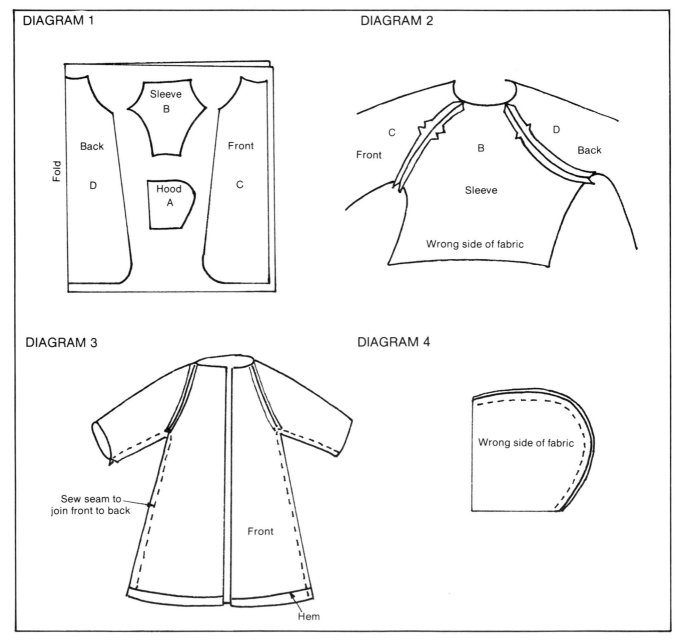

DIAGRAM 1

Sleeve
B

Back

Fold

Front

D

Hood
A

C

DIAGRAM 2

C

Front

B

D

Back

Sleeve

Wrong side of fabric

DIAGRAM 3

Sew seam to join front to back

Front

Hem

DIAGRAM 4

Wrong side of fabric

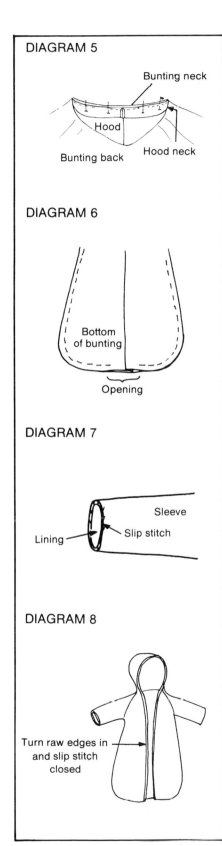

DIAGRAM 5

Bunting neck

Hood

Bunting back

Hood neck

DIAGRAM 6

Bottom
of bunting

Opening

DIAGRAM 7

Sleeve

Lining

Slip stitch

DIAGRAM 8

Turn raw edges in
and slip stitch
closed

6. With right sides facing, pin the front to the back, beginning from the lower edge of one sleeve and continuing to the bottom of the lining. Repeat, beginning under the other sleeve. Stitch the seams with ½-inch seam allowance (Diagram 3). Snip the curves under the arms. Turn the hem of the lining up ¼ inch and press it flat. Turn it up another ½ inch and stitch the hem.

7. With right sides facing, pin the two hood pieces (A) together along the curved edges. Sew them together, leaving a ½-inch seam allowance (Diagram 4). Turn right side out.

8. With the right sides of the fabric facing, pin the lower edge of the hood to the neck edge of the bunting (Diagram 5). Baste the hood in place, remove the pins, and stitch the hood to the bunting, leaving a ½-inch seam allowance. Remove the basting.

9. Repeat steps 5, 6, 7, and 8 with the plaid fabric except omit the hemming step when you stitch the front of the bunting to the back and continue the seam all the way around the curve at the bottom of the bunting, leaving a 3-inch section open in the middle, as shown in Diagram 6. Turn the bunting right side out.

10. Slide the lining, wrong side out, into the bunting. Align the seams with the outer piece and adjust the lining so that it lies completely flat. Turn the raw edges of both the sleeve lining and the outer sleeves to the inside ¼ inch so that the edges are between the two layers of fabric. Pin them in, baste, and slip stitch them closed (Diagram 7). Remove the basting.

Repeat this step, working from the bottom of the lining at the front opening all the way up and around the hood and down the other side (Diagram 8).

11. Turn the bunting wrong side out. To sew the opening closed at the bottom, fold the raw edges of the plaid fabric on the two front pieces back ¼ inch and baste them flat (Diagram 9). Overlap the folded edges at the bottom ½ inch and stitch a seam across the 3-inch opening (Diagram 9A).

Turn the bunting right side out. Slip stitch the front opening closed from the bottom up 7½ inches, as shown in Diagram 10.

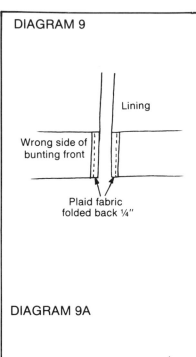

DIAGRAM 9

Lining

Wrong side of
bunting front

Plaid fabric
folded back ¼″

DIAGRAM 9A

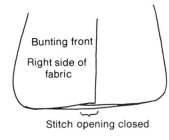

Bunting front

Right side of
fabric

Stitch opening closed

DIAGRAM 10

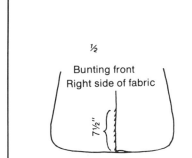

½

Bunting front
Right side of fabric

7½″

12. Using thread to match your fabric, topstitch a row of stitching ½ inch in from the outer edge all the way around the front opening and the hood of the bunting. Sew another row of topstitching around the hood ⅛ inch in from the outer edge, as shown in Diagram 11.

13. Between the rows of topstitching, make two slits in the seam that holds the hood to the bunting (Diagram 12).

Pin the safety pin to one end of the ribbon. Push the pin into one of the slits, work it all the way around the hood casing, and bring it out the other slit. Remove the safety pin. Pull the ribbon ends so that they extend evenly and tie a knot in each end. Evenly space the snaps along the front placket and sew them in place. Turn the sleeves back about 1½ inches so that the contrasting lining is displayed.

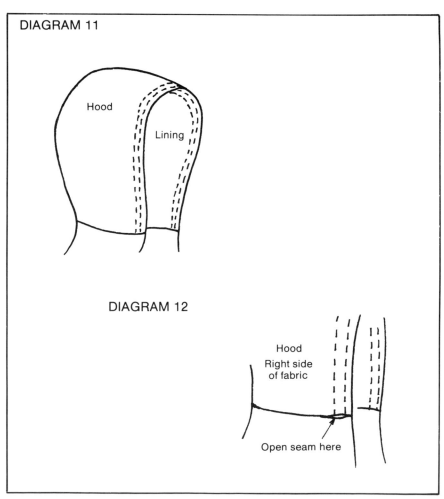

DIAGRAM 11

Hood

Lining

DIAGRAM 12

Hood
Right side
of fabric

Open seam here

BY THE CHILDREN

SUNNY COFFEE-CAN ORGANIZER

Let your child put together this handy organizer to keep his crayons and small toys in. This organizer can serve many purposes. Use it on your countertop in the kitchen to hold cooking utensils, as a caddy for your yarns and needlework, in the office to hold all sorts of supplies, or turn it on its side to become space-saving cubbyholes. Use our sunny yellow and blue combination, or make the organizer to go with your own color scheme.

MATERIALS

6 coffee cans, 1-pound size
small can of gloss-finish spray paint in color of your
    choice
wood saw
12 wooden clothespins
sandpaper for wood, medium-grade
small amount of latex paint in color to contrast with
    spray paint above
small paintbrush
1½ yards ribbon, 1 inch wide, in color to coordinate with
    latex paint above

PROCEDURE

1. Wash and dry the coffee cans; throw away the plastic lids. Turn the coffee cans open side down, and spray-paint them according to the directions on the can. Allow the paint to dry.

2. Saw the tops off the wooden clothespins about ½ inch above the split (Diagram 1) and throw away the top pieces. Sand the top edge lightly with the sandpaper.

3. Paint the clothespins with the paintbrush and the latex paint. Allow the paint to dry thoroughly.

4. Clip the cans together with the clothespins at the top edges, as shown in the project photograph.

5. Tie the ribbon in a bow around the six cans to hold them together, following the project photograph for placement of the ribbon.

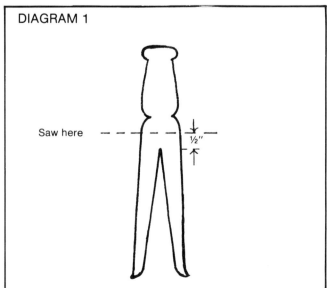

DIAGRAM 1

Saw here   ½"

SEASHELL MOBILE

Take yourself for a walk on a deserted beach at dusk to collect some pretty seashells and then make this breezy mobile as a reminder of that pleasant environment. You can make a more elaborate mobile by adding more seashells and using several different sizes of embroidery hoops, arranging them so that the largest hoop is at the top and the smallest at the bottom, for a tiered effect.

MATERIALS

scissors
ruler
5 yards satin ribbon, ⅛ inch wide, in ecru
wooden embroidery hoop, 6 inches in diameter
plastic ring, ¾ inch in diameter
five seashells
white glue
toothpick

PROCEDURE

1. Cut two pieces of ribbon, each 36 inches long. Set the remaining ribbon aside.

2. Remove the inside hoop from the set of embroidery hoops—this is the one you will use.

3. Pass one end of each of the two 36-inch pieces of ribbon through the plastic ring and adjust them so that the four ends of the ribbon hang down evenly. Tie them in a knot to the ring, as shown in Diagram 1.

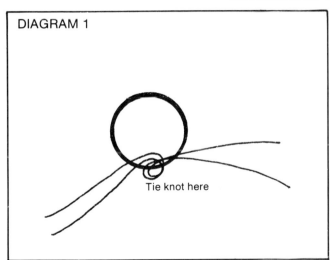

DIAGRAM 1

Tie knot here

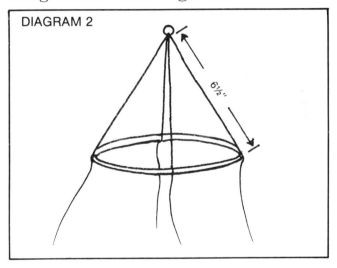

DIAGRAM 2

6½"

4. Tie the four pieces of ribbon equally spaced around the wooden hoop about 6½ inches below the plastic ring, as shown in Diagram 2.

5. Knot each ribbon around a shell, adjusting the length of each ribbon according to the weight of the shell so that when the four outer shells have been added, the hoop will hang evenly.

6. Using the toothpick, place a dot of glue under the part of the ribbon that is tied around each shell and cut off the ends of the ribbon near the knots.

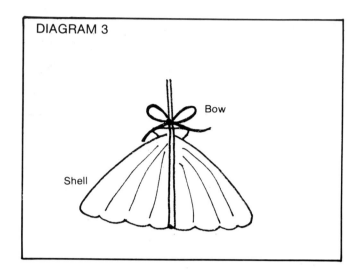

7. Cut four pieces of ribbon, each 10 inches long, and use each to tie a bow around each of the four knots, as shown in Diagram 3.

8. Cut a piece of ribbon 16 inches long. Tie a shell to one end of the ribbon, and put a dot of glue with the toothpick under the ribbon where it ties around the shell. Tie the other end to the plastic ring at the top of the mobile.

9. Cut a piece of ribbon 10 inches long. Tie it in a bow around the knot holding the center shell.

10. Cut a piece of ribbon 10 inches long and tie it into a bow around the five strands of ribbon at the top of the mobile just under the plastic ring.

MUSHROOM-BASKET CENTERPIECE

Dress up a mushroom basket with country-plaid gingham ribbon and it becomes more than just a mushroom basket—it becomes a very decorative centerpiece for any table. We have filled ours with baby's breath for a pretty autumn display, but you could fill yours with pinecones or pile it high with fruit, gourds, or seashells.

MATERIALS

mushroom basket
wood stain in a dark shade
rag
2 yards plaid ribbon, 1 inch wide (we used a cotton
    gingham ribbon)
white glue

PROCEDURE

1. Stain the basket inside and out with the wood stain by rubbing the stain into the wood with the rag.

2. Fold the ribbon in half lengthwise with wrong sides facing.

3. Center the ribbon at the center of the back of the basket and glue one side to the top edge, working each end around to the center front (Diagram 1).

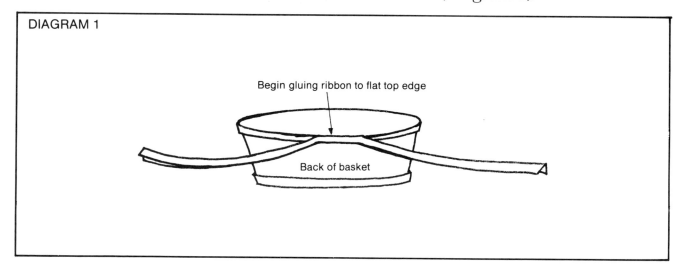

DIAGRAM 1

Begin gluing ribbon to flat top edge

Back of basket

4. Unfold the extra ribbon and tie it into a bow at the front of the basket.

5. Fill the basket with pinecones, gourds, or other natural treasures.

CALICO COLLAGE

Here is a project that encourages its young maker to let his imagination run free to design his own scene—the photograph of our collage should be used only as a sample. Helping the child with the project until he understands the procedure might be a good idea, especially with the fabric-fusing step.

147

MATERIALS

piece of heavy cardboard
ruler
pencil
scissors
piece of white paper
scraps of fabric for background and parts of the picture
white glue
masking tape
about 1 yard fabric fuser (such as Jiffy Fuse or Stitch
  Witchery)
scraps of trims, lace, fabrics, and small buttons for
  wheels and flowers
picture frame (optional)

PROCEDURE

1. Cut a piece of cardboard to the size you want the finished collage to be. If you want to frame the collage with a ready-made frame, make the collage a standard size, such as 8 by 10 inches or 9 by 12 inches. You may have an old frame on hand that could be refinished or renewed with a fresh coat of paint.

2. Cut a piece of white paper the same size as the cardboard. Draw a picture on the paper, using simple shapes so that it will be easy to cut them out of fabric later (we used houses, trees, clouds, and grass).

3. Choose a fabric for the background of the collage that will contrast nicely with the other parts of the picture when they are glued on (we used blue to look like the sky). Cut the fabric 2 inches larger than the cardboard all around.

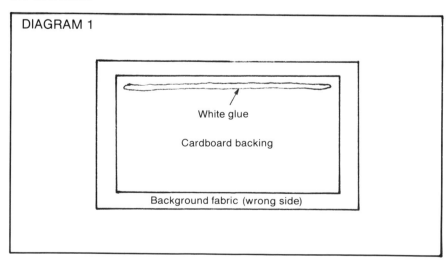

DIAGRAM 1

White glue

Cardboard backing

Background fabric (wrong side)

4. If the background fabric you have chosen is wrinkled, press it flat. Place the fabric on a flat surface, wrong side up. Place the cardboard in the center of the fabric (Diagram 1).

5. Spread a line of white glue along the upper edge of the cardboard (Diagram 1). Fold the fabric over the glue (Diagram 2) and press it down until the glue starts to dry and the fabric stays flat.

6. Turn the cardboard and fabric around so that the opposite edge is up. Pulling the fabric as tight as possible without bending the cardboard, repeat gluing, folding, and drying. Repeat this with the side edges, folding the corners flat as you work.

7. To reinforce the glue, tape the fabric to the cardboard on all four sides (Diagram 3).

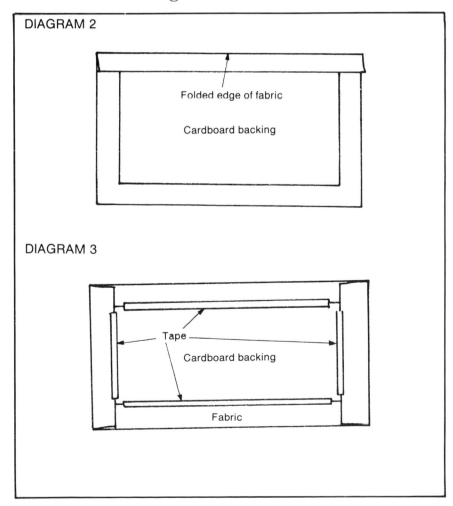

DIAGRAM 2

Folded edge of fabric

Cardboard backing

DIAGRAM 3

Tape

Cardboard backing

Fabric

8. Cut out the shapes of the picture you drew on the white paper. These are the patterns for the parts of the picture.

9. Choose the fabric scraps you will use for each part of the picture and join them with the fabric fuser, following the instructions on the package (fabric fuser helps prevent the edges from fraying).

10. Place one of the patterns, right side up, on the fused fabric. Trace around the pattern with the pencil. Cut the fabric out on the line you have drawn. Now you have one of the fabric pieces you will glue to the background. Set this piece aside and repeat this step with the rest of the shapes.

11. Place the shapes on the background, moving them around until they are exactly where you want them to be. Carefully lift one shape and spread a thin layer of glue on the back. Press the piece in place on the background. Repeat this step with the rest of the shapes.

12. Now add the details to the picture, using the trims you have collected. Make button "flowers," rickrack or lace "fences," ribbon "walks," etc. Glue each trim in place wherever it pleases you.

13. Your collage is now ready for framing. Use a new, bright plastic frame or an old one gaily painted or refinished.

5

BERIBBONED BAND BOXES

Our wallpaper-covered band boxes are takeoffs on the boxes used to store celluloid collars and cuffs long ago. We've used leftover wallpapers and pretty ribbons to trim the boxes, which are perfect for holding all kinds of odds and ends or even as gift wrapping for small presents. The directions we give are to make the larger box, which is from a 2-pound-size oatmeal box. To make the smaller box shown in the photograph, simply use a 1-pound box and adjust the measurements.

MATERIALS

empty oatmeal box, 2-pound size
piece of oaktag, 9 by 18 inches
pencil
scissors
ruler
white glue
wallpaper paste
about 1 yard wallpaper
1½ yards ribbon, 1 inch wide, in color or print to
    coordinate with wallpaper

PROCEDURE

1. Remove the lid from the oatmeal box and throw it away.

2. Cut off the top part of the oatmeal box 6 inches up from the bottom (Diagram 1).

3. Place the bottom of the oatmeal box on the oaktag and trace around it with the pencil. Cut out the circle just outside the pencil line so that you will have a round piece for the lid that is slightly larger in diameter than the box, enabling it to slip over the box when covered with the wallpaper.

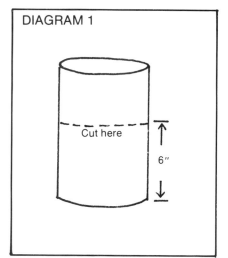

DIAGRAM 1

Cut here

6"

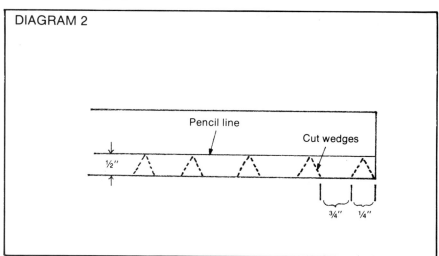

DIAGRAM 2

Pencil line

Cut wedges

½"

¾"   ¼"

4. Cut a strip of oaktag 1¾ by 18 inches. Draw a pencil line along the length of the strip ½ inch down from one edge (Diagram 2).

5. Cut a wedge out of the strip every ¾ inch, making the widest point of each wedge about ¼ inch and then tapering it to a point, as shown in Diagram 2. Fold the wedges up along the pencil line.

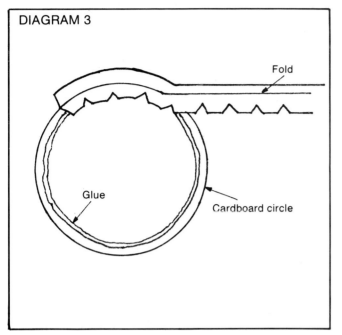

DIAGRAM 3

Fold

Glue

Cardboard circle

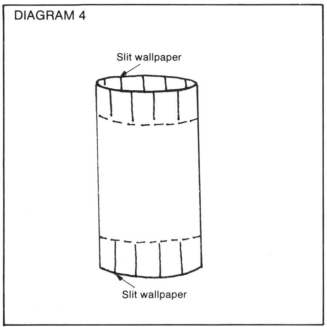

DIAGRAM 4

Slit wallpaper

Slit wallpaper

6. Place a line of glue around the piece for the lid about ¼ inch in from the edge. Glue the wedged-edge of the strip all the way around the top piece, as shown in Diagram 3. Overlap the ends slightly and glue them together. Set the lid aside.

7. Mix a small amount of wallpaper paste. Cut a piece of wallpaper 8 by 18 inches. Apply the paste to the wrong side of the wallpaper. Centering the wallpaper around the outside of the oatmeal box so that the top and bottom edges extend slightly above the top edge and below the bottom edge of the box, paste it around the container.

8. Cut slits into the edge of the wallpaper to the box every ¾ inch around the top and bottom edges, as shown in Diagram 4.

Fold the edge of the wallpaper around the top of the box to the inside and paste it in place. Fold the edge of the wallpaper around the bottom and paste it flat to the bottom of the box.

9. Place the bottom of the box on a piece of the wallpaper and trace around it with the pencil. Cut out the circle, apply wallpaper paste to the wrong side, and paste it to the outside bottom of the box.

10. Now work with the lid to the box. Cut a strip of wallpaper 2½ by 18 inches. Apply wallpaper paste to the wrong side. Centering the strip around the outside of the lid so that the top and bottom edges extend slightly above the lid and below the bottom edge, paste it around the top.

11. Cut slits into the edge of the wallpaper to the lid every ¾ inch around the top and bottom edges.

12. Fold the edge of the wallpaper around the top of the box over the top edge and glue it to the top of the lid. Fold the edge of the wallpaper around the bottom to the inside of the lid and glue it to the inside along the bottom edge.

13. Place the lid to the box on a piece of wallpaper and trace around it with the pencil. Cut out the circle, apply wallpaper paste to the wrong side, and paste it to the outside top of the lid.

14. Cut a piece of ribbon 19 inches long. Turn the bottom of the box over and glue the center section of the ribbon to the center of the bottom (Diagram 5). Bring the ends up the sides of the box, over the top edges, and glue them to the inside of the box.

15. Cut two pieces of ribbon, each 14 inches long. Glue one end of each piece to opposite inside edges of the lid of the box. Bring the ribbons up over the lid and tie them in a bow on the top in the center.

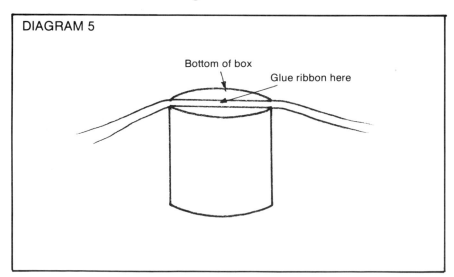

DIAGRAM 5

Bottom of box

Glue ribbon here

6

CALICO-COVERED SWEETHEART FRAME

Frame a cherished photograph of a loved one with this heart-shaped, cutout frame that measures about 6 by 6 inches. Make your frame as pretty as your picture by choosing fabric to complement the colors and theme of your picture. This simple project, which requires only a little bit of fabric and small pieces of cardboard, makes a nice gift for many occasions.

MATERIALS

brown wrapping paper or other paper for cutting
    pattern
ruler
pencil
scissors
tape
piece of heavy cardboard, 11 by 13 inches
4 pieces fabric, 2 pieces 7½ by 7½ inches each and 2
    pieces 3 by 6 inches each
white glue
fabric marker (optional)
1 yard rickrack, standard size, in color to contrast with
    fabric
4 inches grosgrain ribbon, ½ inch wide, in color to
    contrast with fabric
photograph, about 4 by 4 inches

PROCEDURE

1. Using the brown wrapping paper, ruler, and pencil,
enlarge the pattern pieces (see p. 13). Cut the pieces out
of the paper, also cutting the heart shape out of the
piece marked "front." Tape the pieces to the cardboard.
Trace around them and cut the pieces out of the
cardboard. Remove the paper.

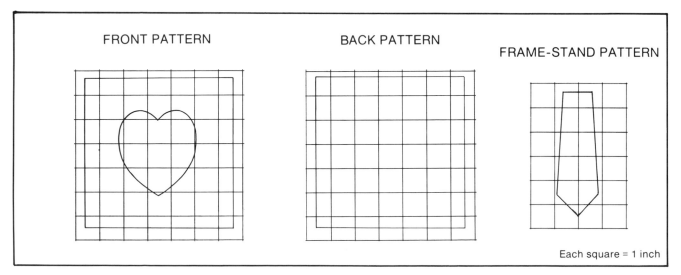

FRONT PATTERN   BACK PATTERN   FRAME-STAND PATTERN

Each square = 1 inch

2. Place one of the 7½-inch squares of fabric on a flat
surface, wrong side up. Center the cardboard square
marked "back" on the fabric. Spread a line of white glue
around the four edges of the cardboard. Fold the fabric
on one side over the glue and press it down, as shown in
Diagram 1.

Fold the fabric on the opposite side over the glue and press it down. Wait a few minutes for the glue to dry.

3. Being sure to fold the corners neatly and flat, fold the remaining edges over the glue and press down, adding an extra dot of glue at each corner under the fabric fold, as shown in Diagram 2, if necessary.

4. Place the other fabric square on a flat surface, wrong side up. Center the cardboard square marked "front" on the fabric. Follow steps 2 and 3 to glue the fabric around the cardboard.

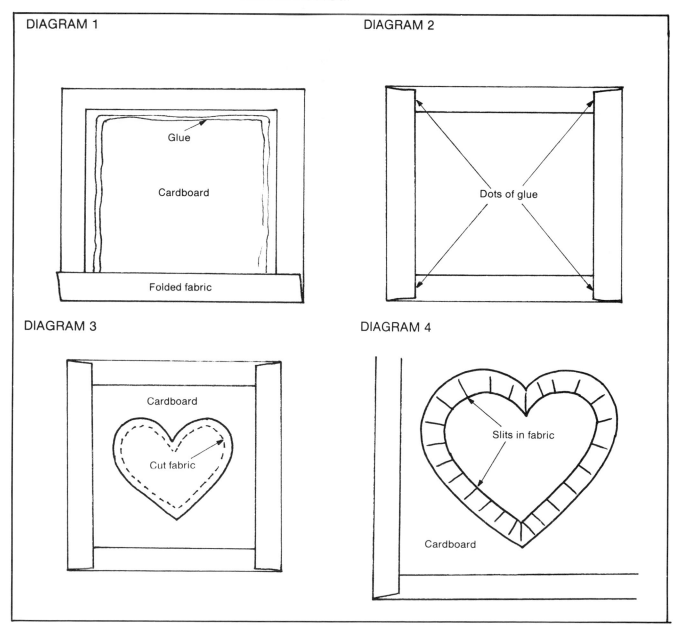

DIAGRAM 1

Glue

Cardboard

Folded fabric

DIAGRAM 2

Dots of glue

DIAGRAM 3

Cardboard

Cut fabric

DIAGRAM 4

Slits in fabric

Cardboard

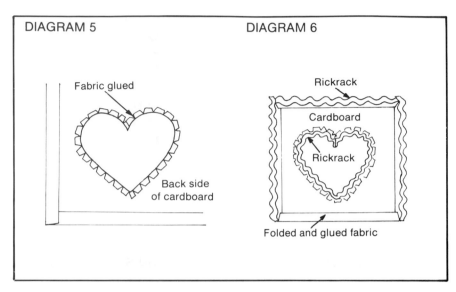

DIAGRAM 5　　　　　　　　　　DIAGRAM 6

Fabric glued

Back side
of cardboard

Rickrack

Cardboard

Rickrack

Folded and glued fabric

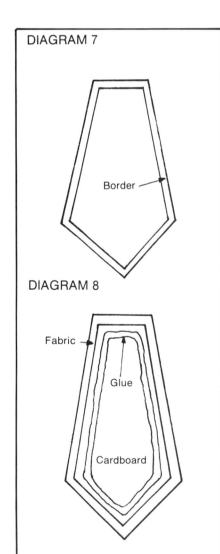

DIAGRAM 7

Border

DIAGRAM 8

Fabric

Glue

Cardboard

5. With the wrong side of the front piece facing up, draw a line on the fabric ½ inch inside the cutout heart shape. Cut the fabric along the line you have drawn, as shown in Diagram 3.

6. Make a number of slits in the fabric extending beyond the cardboard heart up to the cardboard, as shown in Diagram 4.

Spread a line of glue on the cardboard around the heart shape near the edge. Fold the fabric to the inside of the heart shape, over the glue (Diagram 5), stretching the fabric as tightly as you can so that it will be smooth on the front.

7. Cut three pieces of rickrack, each 7 inches long. With the front of the frame wrong side up, spread a line of glue along the two sides and across the top near the edges. Lay one piece of rickrack over the glue on the top edge and one piece down each of the side edges (Diagram 6), placing them so that the points extend beyond the edges of the frame and are visible when you turn over the front piece. Using the same procedure, glue the remaining piece around the edge of the heart shape.

8. With the front piece still wrong side up, spread a line of glue on top of the three pieces of rickrack. Place the wrong side of the fabric-covered backing over it and place it on a flat surface. Lay a heavy book on top of the frame to press together the pieces and allow time for the glue to dry.

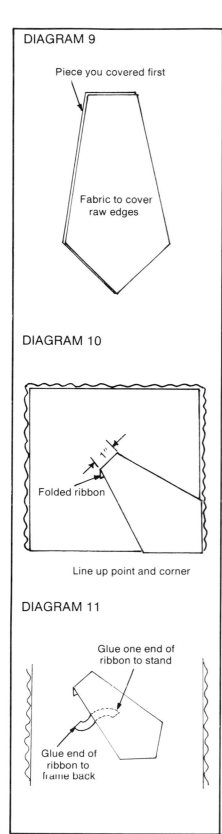

DIAGRAM 9

Piece you covered first

Fabric to cover
raw edges

DIAGRAM 10

1"

Folded ribbon

Line up point and corner

DIAGRAM 11

Glue one end of
ribbon to stand

Glue end of
ribbon to
frame back

9. In the meantime, place one of the remaining pieces of fabric wrong side up, and center the cardboard piece for the frame stand on the fabric. With the fabric marker or a pencil, trace around the cardboard and cut the fabric along this line. Place the cardboard piece on the wrong side of the remaining piece of fabric and trace around the cardboard again. Add ¼ inch all around the line and cut the fabric piece out (Diagram 7).

10. Place the piece of fabric with the ¼-inch border wrong side up on a flat surface. Center the cardboard piece for the frame stand on it. Spread a line of glue around the outer edge of the cardboard (Diagram 8).

11. Making sure that the corners are neat and flat, fold the edges of the fabric over the glued edge and press them down. Add an extra dot of glue at each corner if necessary. Spread a line of glue around the outer edge of the frame stand again, this time on top of the fabric you have just folded and glued. Lay the remaining fabric shape on top of the cardboard and press in place to hide the raw edges of the first piece—this side will be the wrong side (Diagram 9). The frame stand should be completely covered with fabric.

12. Cut a piece of the ribbon 1 inch long and fold it in half lengthwise. With the pointed end of the stand lined up with the lower right-hand corner of the frame, glue one long edge of the ribbon piece to the narrow, top edge of the frame stand on the wrong side and the other half to the back of the frame (Diagram 10).

13. Glue about ½ inch of one end of the remaining piece of ribbon about 2 inches down from the top of the back of the frame stand in the center of its width, with the glued end pointing toward the lower right-hand corner of the frame. Glue about ½ inch of the same side of the other end to the back of the frame itself about 2½ inches up, measured diagonally, from the lower right-hand corner, again with the glued end pointing toward the lower corner (Diagram 11).

14. Slide a picture into the opening at the bottom of the frame.

INDEX